FRENCH

FRENCH

easy recipes • techniques • ingredients

MURDOCH BOOKS

contents

The glorious food of France   6

appetizers and soups   8

*From the simplest of spreads, such as aïoli and tapenade,
to classic, stock-based soups and a suprisingly easy terrine,
elegant French menu-openers are delightfully varied.*

light meals   40

*Humble ingredients such as eggs, cheese and vegetables make
unfussy yet satisfying meals. Enhanced by herbs, garlic or cream,
these transform into classics of the French repertoire.*

main courses   70

*Recipes for poultry, fish and various meats derive from
French home-cooking, using achievable techniques
and ingredients that are accessible.*

vegetables and salads   124

*Give 'everyday' vegetables that French touch by transforming
them into gratins, tians, purées or braises. Create refined
salads using leaves, nuts, herbs and flavoursome dressings.*

desserts   154

*Leave room for dessert! When the sweet course is a
chocolate mousse, a crisp, flaky pastry, or any number of luxuriant
baked custards such as crème brûlée, how could one not?*

The glorious food of France

France is synonymous with many things — wonderful art and architecture, legendary clothing designers, chic citizens, a beautiful language, gorgeous towns and countryside and ... incredible food. More, perhaps, than that of any other nation in the world, the food of France is regarded as a culinary pinnacle. From the simple sophistication of breakfast-time croissants and brioche, to savoury pâtés and artisanal charcuterie, from silky sauces, airy soufflés, delicate crêpes, creamy hand-crafted cheeses and ethereal mousses, tarts, gâteaux and homey baked desserts, French cooking is masterful and, like the people themselves, stylish. A common misconception, however, is that French food is difficult to cook, relying on expensive ingredients and the skills of professional chefs. France is, indeed, the home of *haute cuisine* but this refined style of cooking, evolved from the kitchens of the old aristocracy, is just a small part of the story. The true heart of French cuisine is to be found in *la cuisine du terroir*, the regionally varied, simple fare which has been enjoyed for centuries, and *la cuisine bourgeousie*, which developed from the cooking of French middle classes into the typical bistro fare we recognise today.

France is a large country, spanning diverse landscapes, climatic conditions, historical and cultural traditions, dialects and customs. In the South, the influence of the Mediterranean holds distinct sway. Provence, which typifies for many the France of their dreams, has a rustic cuisine where olives, pungent herbs, olive oil, simply cooked meats and fish, tomatoes, artichokes, fennel, capers and anchovies are common themes. Over in the Pays Basque area, which enjoys proximity to both the Atlantic and the Pyrenees, saffron, dried chilli, tuna and squid, pungent sheep's cheese and chickpeas are common. Contrast this with the cuisine of Brittany and Normandy in France's northwest, lands that produce some of the world's finest dairy and apple products. Here the cooking is enriched with butter and cream-based sauces, cider and calvados, while salt-marsh lamb, clams and mussels, and sweet treats also feature. Then there's the cooking of the German-fringed regions of Alsace and Lorraine, where Kugelhopf, spatzle and choucroute reign supreme.

Although so varied, there are certain constants in everyday French cuisine; namely the use of fresh, seasonal produce, good-quality ingredients and the employment of relatively simple techniques. With the desire of so many modern cooks being to prepare food according to these same principles, this is an opportune time to discover (or, for some, to rediscover) the timeless joys of cooking French.

appetizers and soups

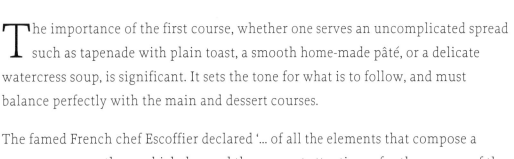

The importance of the first course, whether one serves an uncomplicated spread such as tapenade with plain toast, a smooth home-made pâté, or a delicate watercress soup, is significant. It sets the tone for what is to follow, and must balance perfectly with the main and dessert courses.

The famed French chef Escoffier declared '... of all the elements that compose a menu, soups are those which demand the severest attention ... for the success of the rest of the dinner depends largely on the impression, good or bad, that they have produced on the guest'. The same could be said of an appetizer too — open a meal with a sensational starter and everyone will sit at your table in happy expectation of what is to follow.

The selection featured in this chapter is a wonderful representation of the simpler, more rustic dishes the French often serve at the opening of a lunch or dinner. As such, they are versatile offerings — aïoli will pair happily with either a selection of blanched or raw vegetables, cold poached fish, cooled steamed mussels or crisp salad leaves. Spread anchoïade on croutons and pass them with drinks, or spoon it into a bowl and serve as a dip with a platter of blanched asparagus spears and carrot batons. Leek and potato soup (this is the famous vichyssoise) can be served piping hot or refreshingly chilled, making it perfect year-round fare. Rich bourride can span two courses if you serve the fish pieces separate to the broth; and the brightly flavoured soup called pistou, chunky with seasonal vegetables and dried beans, can be both an appetite-sparking entrée or as a more generous serve in a large bowl with plenty of accompanying bread and butter — a complete, light meal. Charcuterie, or 'cooked meat products' are an important part of the French diet — these encompass sausages, specially cured hams, pâtés and terrines — and often feature at the start of a meal. Generally, charcuterie items are made by specialists and sold in dedicated shops. However, simple varieties of terrines and pâtés are easy and rewarding to make at home, and are a great way to provide an entrée for a large crowd; a pâté or terrine would not be out of place on the Christmas table, for example.

Chicken liver pâté

Although chicken liver pâté is something of a culinary cliché, consider how laborious making it would have been before the age of electric gadgets. Once, pushing through a sieve was required to achieve its silky texture; luckily, we can now whip it up at the flick of a switch.

chicken livers	500 g (1 lb 2 oz)
brandy	4 tablespoons
unsalted butter	90 g (3¼ oz)
onion	1, finely chopped
garlic	1 clove, crushed
thyme	1 teaspoon, chopped
thick (double/heavy) cream	3 tablespoons
white bread	4 slices

Trim the chicken livers, cutting away any discoloured bits and veins. Rinse them, pat dry with paper towels and cut in half. Place in a small bowl with brandy. Cover and refrigerate for a few hours. Drain the livers, reserving the brandy.

Melt half of the butter in a frying pan. Add the onion and garlic and cook over low heat until the onion is soft and transparent. Add the livers and thyme and stir over medium heat until the livers change colour. Add the reserved brandy and simmer for 2 minutes. Cool for 5 minutes.

Place the livers and liquid in a food processor and process until smooth. Add the remaining butter, chopped, and process again until smooth. Pour in the cream and process until just incorporated. Alternatively, roughly mash the livers with a fork, then push them through a sieve and stir in the melted butter and cream.

Season pâté to taste and spoon into a ceramic dish, smoothing the surface. Cover and refrigerate until firm. If the pâté is to be kept for more than a day, chill it and then pour clarified butter over the surface to seal.

To make Melba toasts, preheat the grill (broiler) and cut the crusts off the bread. Toast the bread under the grill on both sides and serve with the pâté.

Cook the livers in a saucepan until just changed in colour.

Spoon the pâté into a dish then smooth the surface using a knife.

Aïoli

Home-made garlic mayonnaise, or aïoli, is a revelation. It is easy to make and, when served with an array of raw and cooked vegetables, makes a sensational appetizer. It can also be spooned over poached chicken or beef and is sometimes stirred into fish soups.

egg yolks	4
garlic	8 cloves, crushed
salt	½ teaspoon
lemon juice	2 tablespoons
olive oil	500 ml (17 fl oz/2 cups)

crudités

baby carrots	6, trimmed with stalks left on
asparagus	6, trimmed and blanched
green beans	6, trimmed and blanched
button mushrooms	6, halved
yellow capsicum (pepper)	1, seeded and cut into batons
red capsicum (pepper)	1, seeded and cut into batons
cauliflower florets	6
fennel bulb	1, cut into batons

Put the egg yolks, garlic, salt and half the lemon juice in a mortar and pestle or food processor and pound or process until light and creamy.

Add the oil, drop by drop at first from the tip of a teaspoon, whisking constantly until it begins to thicken, then add the oil in a thin, steady stream. If you're using a food processor, pour in the oil in a thin stream with the motor running. Season, add the remaining lemon juice and, if necessary, thin with a little warm water.

Arrange the crudités on a large platter and serve the aïoli in a bowl. Store aïoli in the refrigerator for up to three weeks, with a piece of plastic wrap placed directly on the surface to prevent a skin from forming.

It is crucial to whisk the mixture constantly as you add the oil.

Initially, add the oil slowly or the sauce may separate.

Anchoïade

This simple mixture, pungent with the flavours of anchovy and garlic, is an archetypal dish from Provence. There, it is used as a dip for crudités, a filling for savoury pastries or as a spread for small, dry toasts — either way, it's the perfect accompaniment to an aperitif.

anchovy fillets	80 g (2¾ oz) in oil
garlic	2 cloves
black olives	14, pitted
tomato	1, roughly chopped
thyme	1 teaspoon
flat-leaf (Italian) parsley	3 teaspoons chopped
olive oil	1 teaspoon
baguette	1, cut into slices

Put anchovies (with their oil), garlic, olives, tomato, thyme, 1 teaspoon chopped parsley and a generous grinding of black pepper in a mortar and pestle or food processor and pound or process until you have a coarse paste. Add a little extra olive oil if paste is very thick (it should have a spreadable consistency).

Preheat the grill (broiler) and toast the baguette slices on both sides until golden brown. To serve, spread the anchoïade over the baguette and sprinkle with the remaining parsley.

Not so much a loaf of bread as a national symbol, the baguette is a relatively new French culinary development, being only a hundred or so years old. Fine white bread became a status symbol during the reign of Louis XIV; in the nineteenth century, this long slim loaf, with its large ratio of crust to crumb, became popular and associated, largely, with Paris. Not all baguettes are born equal though — a good one should have a golden, crisp exterior with pronounced, raised score marks on the crust. The crumb should be springy, cream-coloured and taste sweet, milky and a little nutty. Try to buy baguettes from good as hey bakeries have superior flavour and texture.

Leeks à la grecque

SERVES 4

The 'à la grecque' here is in homage to the Greek method of preparing vegetables using a piquant wine-based marinade laced with plenty of herbs and spices. This has to be made ahead of time so the vegetables take on plenty of flavour. The result is a refreshing start to a summer meal.

extra virgin olive oil	3 tablespoons
white wine	1½ tablespoons
tomato paste (concentrated purée)	1 tablespoon
sugar	¼ teaspoon
bay leaf	1
thyme sprig	1
garlic	1 clove, crushed
coriander seeds	4, crushed
peppercorns	4
leeks	8, white part only, trimmed
lemon juice	1 teaspoon
flat-leaf (Italian) parsley	1 tablespoon, chopped

Put the oil, wine, tomato paste, sugar, bay leaf, thyme, garlic, coriander seeds, peppercorns and 250 ml (9 fl oz/1 cup) water in a large saucepan. Bring to the boil, cover and then simmer for 5 minutes.

Make criss-cross cuts about 3 cm (1¼ in) deep in the cut ends of the leeks. Add the leeks in a single layer and bring to simmering point. Reduce the heat, cover and then cook for 20–30 minutes, or until leeks are tender (pierce with a fine metal skewer). Lift out leeks and put them in a serving dish.

Add lemon juice to the cooking liquid and boil rapidly until the liquid is slightly syrupy. Remove the bay leaf, thyme and peppercorns. Season with salt and pour over the leeks. Serve the leeks cold, sprinkled with chopped parsley.

Trim the green part and roots of the leeks, leaving the roots intact.

Using a knife, make crisscross cuts in the top end of the leeks.

Test the leeks for tenderness with a fine metal skewer.

three ways with cheese

The quality and variety of cheeses in France is legendary — it is said there are more cheeses there than days in the year. Not only do the French enjoy cheese as a separate course during their meals, they are also fond of incorporating it into their cooking. Here are just a few luscious examples: briny oysters blanketed with rich mornay sauce; curd cheese stirred into olive oil and herbs to make a satisfying topping for toast; and gougères, the famous 'cheese puffs' from Burgundy, which are great when served fresh from the oven with a crisp, pre-dinner white wine.

CERVELLE DE CANUT

Beat 500 g (1 lb 2 oz) fromage blanc or curd cheese with a wooden spoon. Add 2 tablespoons olive oil and 1 finely chopped garlic clove and beat into the cheese. Add 2 tablespoons chopped chervil, 4 tablespoons chopped flat-leaf (Italian) parsley, 2 tablespoons chopped chives, 1 tablespoon chopped tarragon and 4 finely chopped French shallots and mix together well. Season and serve with pieces of toast or bread, perhaps after dessert as you would cheese and biscuits. Serves 8.

OYSTERS MORNAY

Shuck 24 oysters, reserving all the liquid. Strain the liquid into a saucepan. Rinse the oysters to remove any grit. Wash and dry the shells. Melt 30 g (1 oz) of butter in another saucepan, add 1 finely chopped French shallot and cook, stirring, for 3 minutes. Stir in 30 g (1 oz/$1/4$ cup) plain (all-purpose) flour to make a roux. Stir over very low heat for 3 minutes without allowing the roux to brown. Remove from the heat. Add 375 ml (13 fl oz/$1^1/_2$ cups) milk gradually, stirring after each addition until smooth. Return to the heat, add a pinch of nutmeg and half a bay leaf. Stirring constantly, bring to a simmer, then cook for 5 minutes. Strain through a fine sieve into a clean saucepan. Heat the oyster liquid in the saucepan to a simmer (add a little water if you need more liquid). Add the oysters and poach for 30 seconds, then remove with a slotted spoon and place the oysters back into their shells. Stir the cooking liquid into the sauce. Add 20 g ($^3/_4$ oz) grated gruyère cheese, 20 g ($^3/_4$ oz) grated parmesan cheese and 20 g ($^3/_4$ oz) butter. Stir until melted into the sauce. Season with salt and pepper. Preheat the grill (broiler). Spoon a little sauce over each oyster, sprinkle with extra parmesan cheese and place under the hot grill for 2–3 minutes, or until golden. Serves 6.

GOUGÈRES

Preheat the oven to 220°C (425°F/Gas 7) and line two baking trays with baking paper. Combine 100 g ($3^1/_2$ oz) unsalted butter, a large pinch of sugar, a large pinch of sea salt and 250 ml (9 fl oz/1 cup) water in a saucepan. Heat slowly until the butter has melted and the mixture just comes to the boil. Add 150 g ($5^1/_2$ oz/$1^1/_4$ cups) plain (all-purpose) flour, then beat the mixture vigorously over medium heat until the mixture forms a smooth shiny paste that comes away from the side of the pan. Transfer the mixture to the bowl of an electric mixer, cool slightly then, beating continuously, add 3 eggs, one at a time and beating well after each addition. Lightly beat 1 egg and add just enough to the paste so it falls heavily from a spoon — you may not need all the egg. Stir in 100 g ($3^1/_2$ oz) gruyère cheese then drop slightly heaped teaspoons of mixture 4 cm ($1^1/_4$ in) apart onto prepared trays. Bake for 18 minutes, then turn off the heat and leave the gougères to cool in the oven. Serve warm. Gougères are best served on day of making. Makes 36.

cervelle de canut

Tapenade

SERVES 6

You can buy jars of tapenade from the supermarket but it takes very little effort to make it yourself and the results, as with most home-made edibles, are far superior. There are many variations on this savoury paste but olives, capers and anchovies are essential.

black olives	225 g (8 oz) pitted
capers	3 tablespoons, rinsed
anchovy fillets	8
garlic	1 clove, crushed
olive oil	185 ml (6 fl oz/¾ cup)
lemon juice	1 tablespoon
dijon mustard	2 teaspoons
thyme	1 teaspoon chopped
flat-leaf (Italian) parsley	1 tablespoon chopped

Put the olives, capers, anchovies and garlic in a mortar and pestle or a food processor and pound or process until a coarse paste forms.

Add the olive oil, lemon juice, mustard and herbs and pound or process until you have a fairly rough paste.

Serve with bread or crudités for dipping. Store tapenade in the refrigerator for up to three days, covered with plastic wrap.

Olives grow in sunny, dry areas such as the Southern regions of France; here the distinctive, silvery-leafed trees are a common feature of the landscape. Unsurprisingly, olives, both green and black, are much used in the cooking of the South where they feature in salads, spreads, stews or simply as a snack. Olives are inedible straight from the tree; they must go through a lengthy process of curing in brine before they are palatable. They are most commonly purchased in jars, still in their brine. The easiest way to remove the stones from olives is by using a cherry pitter, although you can also crush each olive with the side of a heavy knife and retrieve the stone from the smashed flesh.

Artichokes vinaigrette

The French understand that fine produce just needs some careful preparation and understated embellishing to shine as here, with this classic presentation for artichokes. Use the best olive oil and vinegar you can find and choose firm, compact artichokes with tight leaves.

lemon	1, juiced
globe artichokes	4
vinaigrette	
olive oil	100 ml (3½ fl oz)
spring onions (scallions)	2, finely chopped
white wine	2 tablespoons
white wine vinegar	2 tablespoons
dijon mustard	¼ teaspoon
sugar	pinch
flat-leaf (Italian) parsley	1 tablespoon, finely chopped

To prepare the artichokes, bring a large saucepan of salted water to the boil and add the lemon juice. Break the stalks from the artichokes, pulling out any strings at the same time. Remove the tough outer leaves and then trim the bases flat. Add artichokes to water and put a small plate on top of them to keep them submerged. Cook at a simmer for 25–30 minutes, or until a leaf from the base comes away easily. (The base will be tender when pierced with a skewer.) Cool under cold running water, then drain upside down on a tray.

To make the vinaigrette, heat 1 tablespoon of the oil in a small saucepan, add the spring onion and cook over low heat for 2 minutes. Leave to cool a little, then add white wine, vinegar, mustard and sugar and gradually whisk in the remaining oil. Season well with salt and pepper and stir in half the parsley.

Place an artichoke on each plate and gently prise it open a little. Spoon the dressing over the top, allowing it to drizzle into the artichoke and around the plate. Pour the remaining dressing into a bowl for dipping the leaves in. Sprinkle each artichoke with parsley.

Eat the leaves one by one, dipping them in the vinaigrette and pulling the flesh off the leaves between your teeth. When you reach the middle, pull off any really small leaves and then use a teaspoon to remove the furry choke. Once you've got rid of the choke, you can eat the tender base, or heart, of the artichoke.

Trim off the outer leaves then cut the bases so they are flat.

Whisk the wine, vinegar, mustard, sugar and oil into the mixture.

Terrine de campagne

SERVES 8

The French excel at making charcuterie, or preserved meat products. Most charcuterie (various sausages, galantines, cured hams, pâtés and the like) are made by specialists but some items, such as this scrumptious rustic terrine, are easy for the home cook to prepare.

lean pork	700 g (1 lb 9 oz), cut into cubes
pork belly	200 g (7 oz), cut into strips
chicken livers	200 g (7 oz), trimmed
bacon slices	100 g (3½ oz), chopped
sea salt	1½ teaspoons
black pepper	½ teaspoon
grated nutmeg	pinch
juniper berries	8, lightly crushed
brandy	3 tablespoons
French shallots	2, finely chopped
egg	1 large, lightly beaten
bay leaves	1 sprig
bacon slices	8

Put the pork, pork belly, chicken livers and chopped bacon in a food processor and roughly chop into small dice (you will need to do this in two or three batches). Alternatively, finely dice the meat with a sharp knife.

Put the diced meat in a large bowl and add the sea salt, pepper, nutmeg, juniper berries and brandy. Mix carefully, then cover and refrigerate for at least six hours, or overnight.

Preheat the oven to 180°C (350°F/Gas 4). Lightly butter a 20 x 7 x 9 cm (8 x 2¾ x 3½ in) terrine or loaf (bar) tin. Add shallots and egg to the marinated meat and mix together.

Put the bay leaves in the base of the terrine tin and then line with the bacon slices, leaving enough hanging over the sides to cover the top. Spoon the filling into the terrine and fold the ends of the bacon over the top. Cover the top with a layer of well-buttered baking paper and then wrap whole terrine in foil.

Place the terrine in a large baking dish and pour hot water into the baking dish to come halfway up the sides of the terrine. Bake for 1½ hours, or until the pâté is shrinking away from the sides of the terrine.

Lift terrine out of the bain-marie and leave the pâté to cool, still wrapped in the paper and foil. Once cold, drain off the excess juices, cover with plastic wrap and refrigerate for up to a week.

Run a knife around the inside of the terrine to loosen the pâté and then turn out onto a board. Serve in slices with baguette.

Bourride

Bourride, like bouillabaisse, is one of the great fish soups of Provence, where it is made with a variety of fish — you can either use several types or, just as successfully, stick to one. A rich soup, thickened as it is with garlicky aïoli, bourride makes a great meal-in-a-bowl.

garlic croutons

baguette	½, day-old, sliced
olive oil	3 tablespoons
garlic	1 clove, halved

aïoli

egg yolks	2
garlic	4 cloves, crushed
lemon juice	4 teaspoons
olive oil	250 ml (9 fl oz/1 cup)

stock

saffron threads	¼ teaspoon
dry white wine	1 litre (35 fl oz/4 cups)
leek	1, white part only, chopped
carrots	2, chopped
onions	2, chopped
orange zest	2 long pieces
fennel seeds	2 teaspoons
thyme sprigs	3
firm white fish such as monkfish, sea bass, cod, perch, sole or bream	2.5 kg (5 lb 8 oz) whole, filleted, skinned and cut into 4 cm (1½ in) pieces (reserve the trimmings)
egg yolks	3

Preheat the oven to 160°C (315°F/Gas 2–3). To make the garlic croutons, brush the bread with oil and bake for 10 minutes, or until crisp. Rub one side of each slice with garlic.

To make the aïoli, put the egg yolks, garlic and 3 teaspoons of the lemon juice in a mortar and pestle or food processor and pound or process until light and creamy. Add the oil, drop by drop, from the tip of a teaspoon, whisking constantly until it begins to thicken, then add oil in a thin, steady stream. (If you're using a processor, pour in the oil in a thin stream with the motor running.) Season, add remaining lemon juice and, if necessary, thin with a little warm water. Cover and refrigerate.

To make the stock, soak the saffron in 1 tablespoon of hot water for 15 minutes. Put the saffron, wine, leek, carrot, onion, orange zest, fennel seeds, thyme and fish trimmings in a large saucepan with 1 litre (35 fl oz/4 cups) water. Cover and bring to the boil, then simmer for 20 minutes, skimming occasionally. Strain into a clean saucepan, pressing the solids with a wooden spoon to extract all the liquid. Bring the stock to a gentle simmer, add half the fish and poach for 5 minutes. Remove and keep warm while cooking the remaining fish, then remove from the pan and bring the stock back to the boil. Boil for 5 minutes, or until slightly reduced, then remove from the heat.

Put half the aïoli and the yolks in a bowl and mix until smooth. Whisk in a ladleful of hot stock, then gradually add 5 ladlefuls, stirring constantly. Pour back into the pan containing the rest of the stock and whisk over low heat for 3–5 minutes, or until the soup is hot and thickened slightly (don't let it boil or it will curdle). Season with salt and pepper.

To serve, put two garlic croutons in each bowl, top with a few pieces of fish and ladle over the hot soup. Serve the remaining aïoli separately.

Leek and potato soup

This is a versatile soup. It can be served piping hot in winter or, in warmer months, chilled; in this latter form it is famously known as vichyssoise. This is a dish far more delicious than its humble ingredients might suggest, with leeks lending sweetness and cream giving the purée a rich finish.

butter	50 g (1¾ oz)
onion	1, finely chopped
leeks	3, white part only, chopped
celery	1 stalk, finely chopped
garlic	1 clove, finely chopped
all-purpose potatoes	200 g (7 oz), peeled and chopped
chicken stock	750 ml (26 fl oz/3 cups)
cream (whipping)	220 ml (7¾ fl oz)
chives	2 tablespoons, roughly chopped
white pepper	pinch

Melt the butter in a large saucepan and add the onion, leek, celery and garlic. Cover and cook, stirring occasionally, over low heat for 15 minutes, or until the vegetables are softened but not browned. Add potato and stock and bring to the boil.

Reduce the heat and leave to simmer, covered, for 20 minutes. Allow to cool a little before puréeing in a blender or food processor. Return to the clean saucepan.

Bring the soup gently back to the boil and stir in the cream. Season with salt and white pepper and reheat without boiling. Serve hot or well chilled, garnished with chives.

Add potato and stock to the vegetables then bring to the boil.

Return puréed soup to a clean saucepan then stir in the cream.

the perfect
french onion soup

Gentle, slow cooking renders onions sweet and meltingly tender; it is vital not to rush the process. French onion soup is another of those dishes that is far more complex in flavour than its few simple ingredients might suggest; it requires attention to the quality of the ingredients as well as the cooking processes to achieve the deep, savoury flavours and silky texture that make it an absolute delight. This soup is best when made with good, home-made brown beef stock.

Melt 50 g (1¾ oz) of butter in a large, heavy-bottomed saucepan, then add 750 g (1 lb 10 oz) finely sliced onions. Cook the onions over low heat for 25 minutes, stirring occasionally, or until the onions are golden and beginning to caramelise. Add 2 finely chopped garlic cloves and 45 g (1½ oz/⅓ cup) plain (all-purpose) flour and stir continuously for 2 minutes. Stirring, gradually add 2 litres (70 fl oz/8 cups) beef or chicken stock and 250 ml (9 fl oz/1 cup) white wine, then bring to the boil. Reduce the heat, add 1 dried bay leaf and 2 thyme sprigs, then cover and simmer over medium–low heat for 25 minutes. Remove the herbs and season to taste. Preheat the grill (broiler). Toast 8 slices of day-old baguette, divide among four warmed soup bowls then ladle over the soup. Sprinkle with 100 g (3½ oz) grated gruyère cheese, then place bowls under the grill until the cheese melts and turns golden. Serves 4.

Watercress soup

As with all the soups in this chapter, it is critical to use a good, home-made chicken stock here. The gorgeous green colour of watercress soup can easily turn an unappealing grey; the best way to avoid this is to serve it as soon after making it as possible.

butter	30 g (1 oz)
onion	1, finely chopped
all-purpose potatoes	250 g (9 oz), diced
chicken stock	600 ml (21 fl oz)
watercress	1 kg (2 lb 4 oz), trimmed and chopped
cream (whipping)	125 ml (4 fl oz/½ cup)
milk	125 ml (4 fl oz/½ cup)
nutmeg	freshly grated, to season
chives	2 tablespoons roughly chopped

Melt butter in a large saucepan and add the onion. Cover and cook over low heat until onion is softened but not browned. Add potato and chicken stock and then simmer for 12 minutes, or until the potato is tender. Add the watercress and then cook for 1 minute.

Remove from the heat and leave the soup to cool a little before pouring into a blender or food processor. Blend until smooth and return to a clean saucepan.

Bring the soup gently back to the boil and stir in the cream and milk. Season with nutmeg, salt and pepper and reheat without boiling. Serve garnished with chives.

Watercress is most commonly regarded as a salad green yet its bright, peppery flavours are ideally suited to soups and purées. Cultivated watercress is best when harvested young during the cooler part of the year, when its flavour will be smooth and mild. A member of the mustard family, watercress can be extremely hot and bitter, so taste before you buy. Choose watercress with small leaves and thin stems — avoid any with thick, flowering stems as the flavour will be very strong. As watercress is a delicate green, store it in a sealed plastic bag in the refrigerator and use as soon after purchase as possible as its flavour, and freshness, will fast diminish.

Garlic soup

SERVES 4

The people of Provence are fond of garlic, as the amount used in this soup will attest. Don't be daunted by the quantities; the egg yolk and potato soften any harsh flavours, as does the initial cooking in oil. What you are left with is a soup perfumed with the sweet, pungent flavours of the garlic.

olive oil	150 ml (5 fl oz)
bacon slices	125 g (4½ oz), finely chopped
garlic	2 bulbs, cloves peeled and roughly chopped
all-purpose potato	1, diced
chicken stock	1.5 litres (52 fl oz/6 cups)
bouquet garni	1
egg yolks	3

cheese croutons

baguette	½, sliced
gruyère cheese	50 g (1¾ oz), grated

Heat 1 tablespoon of the oil in a large heavy-based saucepan and cook the bacon over medium heat for 5 minutes without browning. Add the garlic and potato and cook for 5 minutes, or until softened. Add the stock and bouquet garni, bring to the boil and simmer for 30 minutes, or until the potato starts to dissolve into the soup.

Put the egg yolks in a large bowl and pour in the remaining oil in a thin stream, whisking until thickened. Gradually whisk in the hot soup. Strain back into the saucepan, pressing to extract all the liquid, and heat gently without boiling. Season.

To make the cheese croutons, preheat the grill (broiler) and lightly toast bread on both sides. Sprinkle with the cheese and grill until melted. Place a few croutons in each warm bowl and ladle the soup over the top, or serve the croutons on the side.

Once vegetables are softened, add the bouquet garni and stock.

Whisk the yolks and oil well, then slowly whisk in the hot stock.

Soupe au pistou

As the word suggests, 'pistou' is a close cousin to Italian pesto and can be used in similar ways. Here, the basil-based paste is a crucial component in this mixed-vegetable soup, brightening the appearance and flavour of an already sunny dish.

dried haricot beans	250 g (9 oz)
olive oil	2 teaspoons
onion	1, finely chopped
garlic	2 cloves, crushed
celery	1 stalk, chopped
carrots	3, diced
bouquet garni	1
all-purpose potatoes	4, diced
green beans	150 g (5½ oz) small, chopped
chicken stock	500 ml (17 fl oz/2 cups)
tomatoes	3
zucchini (courgettes)	4, diced
vermicelli noodles	150 g (5½ oz), broken into pieces
peas	150 g (5½ oz), fresh or frozen

pistou

garlic	6 cloves, peeled and chopped
basil	80 g (2¾ oz)
parmesan cheese	100 g (3½ oz), grated
olive oil	200 ml (7 fl oz)

Soak the haricot beans in cold water overnight. Drain, then put in a saucepan and cover with cold water. Bring to the boil, then lower the heat and simmer for 1 hour, or until the beans are tender. Drain well.

To make the pistou, put garlic, basil and parmesan in a mortar and pestle or food processor and pound or process until finely ground. Slowly add the olive oil, pounding constantly with the mortar and pestle. If you are using a food processor, add the oil in a thin stream with the motor running. Mix thoroughly. Cover with plastic wrap and set aside.

Heat the olive oil in a large saucepan. Add the onion and garlic and cook over low heat for 5 minutes, or until softened but not browned. Add the celery, carrot and bouquet garni and cook for 10 minutes, stirring occasionally. Add the potato, green beans, chicken stock and 1.75 litres (61 fl oz/7 cups) water and simmer for 10 minutes.

Score a cross in the base of each tomato. Plunge into boiling water for 20 seconds, then drain and peel the skin away from the cross. Chop tomatoes finely, discarding the cores. Add to the soup with the courgettes, haricot beans, vermicelli and the peas. Cook for 10 minutes or until tender (if you are using frozen peas, add them at the last minute just to heat through). Season and serve with pistou spooned on top.

A mortar and pestle gives the best texture and flavour to pistou.

Vegetables should be cooked through but still have texture.

Savoury tarts, egg and cheese based dishes, as well as simple seafood preparations make wonderful light meals and the French have excelled in the creation of these. Many of the dishes in this chapter, such as piperade, pissaladière or omelette, are classified in French gastronomy as hot hors d'oeuvres and as such, would traditionally be served before a light main course. They are perfectly suited, though, to stand on their own as simple dinners or a weekend brunch, needing little more than an accompanying green salad, crusty bread and perhaps fruit or a simple dessert to follow. Many too are examples of domestic French cookery, as opposed to the haute cuisine or restaurant fare we so often associate with the country. Traditionally, many households had access to their own supplies of freshly laid eggs, farmhouse cheeses and home-grown vegetables so domestic cooks learned to fashion simple, yet satisfying meals from these fresh, everyday ingredients.

Regional variants of crêpes, galettes, pies, omelettes and stuffed vegetables appear all over France; in their original form, some of these dishes were positively ascetic but, over generations and with rising affluence, have been greatly embellished and enriched. Crêpes, for example, which are native to Brittany, were first served as a meatless meal on Fridays, accompanied by nothing more than buttermilk and the region's famed cider; these days crêpes are enjoyed all over France and enclose a huge variety of rich fillings. Quiche, now ubiquitous, has similarly ancient origins. It was originally made with a heavy bread-dough base, according to the Larousse Gastronomique, and, subject to generations of refinement, has become the luscious savoury custard baked in a tender pastry crust we know today. Light, fluffy omelettes and airy soufflés may well be the quintessential French dishes and make excellent, and quickly-assembled, light meals. They demonstrate perfectly that unmistakable French knack for taking a handful of everyday ingredients — eggs, vegetables, milk and some butter — and transforming them into something elegant. The inclusion of seafood or a prime cheese into an omelette or soufflé elevates it into the realms of the truly 'gourmet'.

These dishes rely on easily mastered, but important culinary techniques includingthe making of tender, shrink-resistant pastry, the whisking of egg whites into ethereal foam, the cooking of onions to caramelized softness, the slight undercooking of an omelette so it arrives at the table beautifully creamy in the centre. Once conquered, though, these techniques enable the cook to quickly whip up tasty, smart treats from pantry and refrigerator staples.

Pissaladière

Soft caramelized onions, olives, plenty of anchovies and fresh thyme flavour this delicious tart that originated in Nice. You can serve pissaladière hot or at room temperature as either lunch or casual dinner fare and, as it transports well, it is great to take on a picnic.

bread dough

dried yeast	2 teaspoons
plain (all-purpose) flour	250 g (9 oz/2 cups)
salt	½ teaspoon
olive oil	3 tablespoons
butter	40 g (1½ oz)
olive oil	1 tablespoon
onions	1.5 kg (3 lb 5 oz), thinly sliced
thyme	2 tablespoons
olive oil	1 tablespoon
anchovy fillets	16, halved lengthways
black olives	24, pitted

To make the bread dough, mix the yeast with 120 ml (4 fl oz) of warm water. Leave for 10 minutes in a warm place until the yeast becomes frothy.

Sift flour into a large bowl and add the salt, olive oil and the yeast mixture. Mix until dough clumps together and forms a ball. Turn out onto a lightly floured work surface. Knead the dough, adding a little more flour or a few drops of warm water if necessary, until you have a soft dough that is not sticky but dry to the touch. Knead for 10 minutes, or until smooth, and the impression made by a finger springs back immediately.

Rub inside of a large bowl with olive oil. Roll the ball of dough around in bowl to coat it with oil, then cut a shallow cross on the top of the ball with a sharp knife. Leave dough in the bowl, cover with a tea towel (dish towel) and leave in a draught-free place for 1–1½ hours, or until the dough has doubled in size.

Knock back the dough by punching it with your fist several times to expel the air and then knead it again for a couple of minutes. (At this stage the dough can be stored in the fridge for 4 hours, or frozen. Bring back to room temperature before continuing.) Leave in a warm place to rise until doubled in size.

Melt butter with the olive oil in a saucepan and add onion and half the thyme. Cover saucepan and cook over low heat for 45 minutes, stirring, until onion is softened but not browned. Season and cool. Preheat the oven to 200°C (400°F/Gas 6).

Roll out the bread dough to roughly fit a greased 34 x 26 cm (13½ x 10½ in) shallow baking tray. Brush with the olive oil, then spread with the onion.

Lay anchovies in a lattice pattern over the onion and arrange the olives in the lattice diamonds. Bake for 20 minutes, or until dough is cooked and lightly browned. Sprinkle with remaining thyme leaves and cut into squares. Serve hot or warm.

Roll the dough base around the pin to transfer it to a tray.

Arrange anchovies in a lattice then put olives in the 'diamonds'.

Piperade

SERVES 4

A rustic dish from the Basque region which borders Spain, piperade combines onion, red capsicum (peppers), tomato, ham and eggs to luscious effect. This is satisfying weekend brunch fare. Make this dish in summer when tomatoes and capsicums (peppers) are sweet, plump and full-flavoured.

olive oil	2 tablespoons
onion	1 large, thinly sliced
red capsicums (peppers)	2, seeded and cut into batons
garlic	2 cloves, crushed
tomatoes	750 g (1 lb 10 oz)
cayenne pepper	pinch
eggs	8, lightly beaten
butter	10 g (¼ oz)
ham	4 thin slices

Heat the oil in a large heavy-based frying pan and cook the onion for 3 minutes, or until it has softened. Add the capsicum and garlic. Cover and cook for 8 minutes, stirring, to soften.

Score a cross in the base of each tomato. Plunge into boiling water for 20 seconds, then drain and peel the skin away from the cross. Chop the tomatoes, discarding the cores. Spoon the chopped tomato and cayenne over the pepper, cover the pan and cook for a further 5 minutes.

Remove the lid from frying pan and increase the heat. Cook for 3 minutes or until the juices have evaporated, shaking the pan often. Season well with salt and pepper. Add the eggs and stir into the mixture until combined well and eggs are just cooked.

Meanwhile, heat the butter in a small frying pan and fry the ham. Arrange the ham on the piperade and serve immediately.

Once blanched, skins will easily peel away from the tomatoes.

Add the chopped tomato to the softened capsicums.

Flamiche

Leeks are one of those underrated vegetables that generally play a supporting role in stews, stocks and sauces. However, the French have long appreciated the sweet mildness of well-cooked leeks and here they star in this delicious pie, which is true regional fare from Picardie.

tart pastry	
plain (all-purpose) flour	220 g (7¾ oz/1¾ cups)
salt	pinch
unsalted butter	150 g (5½ oz), chilled and diced
egg yolk	1
leeks	500 g (1 lb 2 oz), white part only, finely sliced
butter	50 g (1¾ oz)
Maroilles (soft cheese)	180 g (6½ oz), chopped (you can also use Livarot or Port Salut)
egg	2, 1 lightly beaten
egg yolk	1
thick (double/heavy) cream	3 tablespoons

To make tart pastry, sift the flour and salt into a large bowl. Add the butter and rub in with your fingertips until mixture resembles breadcrumbs. Add egg yolk and 2–3 teaspoons of cold water and mix with a palette knife until dough just starts to come together. Bring the dough together with your hands and shape into a ball. Wrap in plastic wrap and refrigerate for at least 30 minutes.

Preheat the oven to 180°C (350°F/Gas 4) and put a baking tray on the top shelf. Roll out the pastry on a lightly floured surface. Use three-quarters of the pastry to line the base and sides of a 23 cm (9 inch) fluted loose-based tart tin.

Cook leek for 10 minutes in boiling salted water, then drain. Heat the butter in a frying pan, add the leek and cook, stirring, for 5 minutes. Stir in the cheese. Tip into a bowl and add the egg, egg yolk and cream. Season and mix well.

Pour the filling into the pastry shell and smooth. Roll out the remaining pastry into a round large enough to cover the pie. Pinch the edges together and trim. Cut a hole in the centre and brush egg over the top. Bake for 35–40 minutes on the baking tray until browned. Leave in tin for 5 minutes before serving. Serve warm or at room temperature. Flamiche is best eaten on the day it is made.

Rub the butter into the flour mixture using your fingertips.

Roll the remaining pastry out to cover the tart then trim the edges.

Smoked trout gougère

SERVES 4

Choux pastry isn't difficult to make but it is one of those culinary basics that requires a little practice and patience to master; once you have though, you'll be able to whip up a batch in no time at all. This dish makes a wonderful casual lunch or dinner.

butter	75 g (2½ oz)
plain (all-purpose) flour	120 g (4¼ oz/1 cup), sifted twice
smoked paprika	¼ teaspoon
eggs	3 large, beaten
gruyère cheese	100 g (3½ oz), grated

filling

smoked trout	400 g (14 oz)
watercress	100 g (3½ oz), trimmed
butter	30 g (1 oz)
plain (all-purpose) flour	20 g (¾ oz)
milk	300 ml (10½ fl oz)

Preheat the oven to 200°C (400°F/Gas 6) and put a baking tray on the top shelf.

Melt the butter with 185 ml (6 fl oz/¾ cup) water in a large saucepan, then bring to the boil. Remove from the heat and sift in all the flour and the paprika. Return to the heat and beat continuously with a wooden spoon to make a smooth, shiny paste that comes away from the side of the pan. Allow to cool for a few minutes. Beat in eggs one at a time, until mixture is shiny and smooth; it should drop off the spoon but not be too runny. Stir in two-thirds of the cheese.

Spoon the dough around the edge of a shallow, lightly greased baking dish. Put in the oven on the hot baking tray and cook for 45–50 minutes, or until the choux is well risen and browned.

Meanwhile, to make the filling, peel skin off the trout and lift off the top fillet. Pull out bones, then roughly flake the flesh. Wash the watercress and then put in a large saucepan with just the water clinging to leaves. Cover the pan and steam the watercress for 2 minutes, or until just wilted. Drain, cool and squeeze with your hands to get rid of excess liquid. Roughly chop the watercress.

Melt butter in a saucepan. Stir in the flour to make a roux and cook, stirring, for 3 minutes over very low heat without allowing the roux to brown. Remove from the heat and add the milk gradually, stirring after each addition until smooth. Return to the heat and simmer for 3 minutes. Stir in smoked trout and watercress and season well.

Spoon trout filling into the centre of the cooked choux pastry and return to the oven for 10 minutes, then serve immediately.

Quiche Lorraine

Native to Nancy in the region of Lorraine, quiche lorraine is a triumph of simplicity and is defined by its tender pastry base and the shallow slick of soft, baked savoury custard. This, traditionally, is flavoured with bacon, a hint of nutmeg and no cheese whatsoever.

tart pastry

plain (all-purpose) flour	220 g (7¾ oz/1¾ cups)
salt	pinch
unsalted butter	150 g (5½ oz), chilled and diced
egg yolk	1
butter	25 g (1 oz)
bacon slices	300 g (10½ oz), diced
thick (double/heavy) cream	250 ml (9 fl oz/1 cup)
eggs	3, lightly beaten
nutmeg	freshly grated, to season

To make the tart pastry, sift the flour and salt into a large bowl, add the butter and rub in with your fingertips until the mixture resembles breadcrumbs. Add the egg yolk and 2–3 teaspoons of cold water and mix with the blade of a palette knife until the dough just starts to come together. Bring the dough together with your hands and shape into a ball. Wrap in plastic wrap and refrigerate for at least 30 minutes.

Preheat the oven to 200°C (400°F/Gas 6). Roll out the pastry on a lightly floured surface to fit the base and the sides of a 25 cm (10 in) fluted loose-based tart tin. Line the pastry shell with a crumpled piece of baking paper and uncooked rice or baking beads. Blind bake pastry for 10 minutes, remove the paper and beads and bake for a further 3–5 minutes, or until pastry is just cooked but still very pale. Reduce oven to 180°C (350°F/Gas 4).

Melt the butter in a small frying pan and cook the bacon until golden. Drain on paper towels.

Whisk together the cream and eggs and season with salt, pepper and nutmeg. Scatter the bacon over the pastry shell and then pour in the egg mixture. Bake for 30 minutes, or until the filling is set. Leave in the tin for 5 minutes before serving.

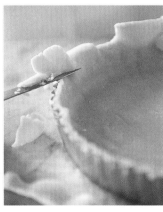

Run a knife around the edge of the pastry to trim it.

Using a jug makes pouring the filling in the pastry case easier.

three ways with eggs

Although the fundamental cooking methods for eggs are few and simple, there are countless ways to present and flavour them. Here, baked in a ramekin with mushrooms, cheese and ham, the versatile egg makes an elegant brunch dish or entrée. Similarly, the croustade casings and dabs of hollandaise for oeufs en croustade, or the silky, sophisticated red wine sauce spooned over poached eggs on toast, elevate the humble egg into something refined and memorable.

OEUFS EN COCOTTE

Preheat the oven to 200°C (400°F/Gas 6) and put a baking tray on the top shelf. Grease four ramekins with 15 g ($^1/_2$ oz) melted butter. Pour 3 tablespoons of cream (whipping) into ramekins and then divide 4 sliced mushrooms, 40 g ($1^1/_2$ oz) sliced ham and 40 g ($1^1/_2$ oz) grated gruyère cheese among the four ramekins. Break an egg into each ramekin. Mix 3 tablespoons of cream (whipping) with 1 tablespoon finely chopped herbs such as chervil, parsley or chives and pour over the top. Bake on the hot baking tray for 15–20 minutes, depending on how runny you like your eggs. Remove from oven while still a little runny as the eggs will continue to cook. Season well and serve immediately with crusty toasted bread. Serves 4.

OEUFS EN CROUSTADE

Preheat the oven to 180°C (350°F/Gas 4). Cut four 3 cm ($1^1/_4$ in) thick slices from a loaf of white bread and remove the crusts. Cut each piece of bread into a 9 cm ($3^1/_2$ in) square, then use a 6.5 cm ($2^1/_2$ in) round cutter to cut a circle in the centre of the bread, without cutting all the way through. Use a knife to scoop out the bread from the centre to form a hollow. Mix together 50 g ($1^3/_4$ oz) melted butter and 1 crushed garlic clove and brush all over the bread. Place on a baking tray and bake for 8 minutes, or until crisp and golden. Keep warm. To make the hollandaise sauce, put 2 egg yolks and 2 teaspoons lemon juice in a saucepan over low heat. Whisk continuously, adding 90 g ($3^1/_4$ oz) cubed butter, piece by piece, until the sauce thickens then season. The sauce should be of pouring consistency; if it is a little too thick, add 1–2 tablespoons of hot water to thin it a little. To poach the eggs, bring a saucepan of water to the boil. Crack an egg into a bowl, reduce the heat and slide the egg into the simmering water. Poach for 3 minutes, then remove with a slotted spoon and drain on paper towels. Poach the remaining eggs. Trim the eggs and place an egg into each croustade. Pour over a little hollandaise sauce and sprinkle with 1 teaspoon finely chopped flat-leaf (Italian) parsley. Serves 4.

POACHED EGGS WITH RED WINE SAUCE

Heat 30 g (1 oz) unsalted butter in a saucepan, add 20 g ($^3/_4$ oz) plain (all-purpose) flour, then stir over medium–low heat for 2 minutes. Whisking constantly, add 750 ml (26 fl oz/3 cups) light red wine, a cup at a time, bringing the mixture to a simmer between additions. Bring the mixture to a gentle simmer. Add 2 thyme sprigs, 1 dried bay leaf and 8 black peppercorns, then cook sauce over low heat for 30 minutes, stirring occasionally. Pour sauce through a fine sieve, discard solids, then return to low heat. Cover and keep warm. Fill a deep frying pan half full with water, add 1 tablespoon red wine vinegar then bring to a gentle simmer. Break in 8 large eggs, a few at a time, then poach in the barely simmering water for 3–4 minutes or until whites are firm but yolks are still soft. Remove with a slotted spoon and drain on paper towels. Meanwhile, heat $2^1/_2$ tablespoons extra virgin olive oil in a saucepan, add 2 chopped onions and 125 g ($4^1/_2$ oz) bacon, rind removed and finely chopped. Cook, stirring often, for 7–8 minutes or until golden. Butter four 1 cm ($^1/_2$ in) thick slices toasted baguette and divide among plates. Spoon the onion mixture over the toasts, top each with an egg then spoon over red wine sauce and serve immediately. Serves 4.

oeufs en cocotte

Crab soufflés

Good fishmongers sell freshly cooked crab meat, taking much of the work out of this dish. Have your guests seated so that as soon as the soufflés come out of the oven, they are ready to both eat and admire their impressive, fully puffed glory.

butter	15 g (½ oz), melted
cloves	2
onion	¼ small
bay leaf	1
black peppercorns	6
milk	250 ml (9 fl oz/1 cup)
butter	15 g (½ oz)
French shallot	1, finely chopped
plain (all-purpose) flour	15 g (½ oz)
egg yolks	3
cooked crab meat	250 g (9 oz)
cayenne pepper	pinch
egg whites	5

Preheat the oven to 200°C (400°F/Gas 6). Brush six 125 ml (4 fl oz/½ cup) ramekins with the melted butter.

Press the cloves into the onion, then put in a small saucepan with the bay leaf, peppercorns and milk. Gently bring to the boil, then remove from heat and leave to infuse for 10 minutes. Strain the milk, discarding solids.

Melt the butter in a heavy-based saucepan, add the shallot and cook, stirring, for 3 minutes until softened but not browned. Stir in the flour to make a roux. Cook, stirring, for 3 minutes over low heat without allowing the roux to brown.

Remove from the heat and add the infused milk gradually, stirring after each addition until smooth. Return to the heat and simmer for 3 minutes, stirring continuously. Remove from the heat and beat in egg yolks, one at a time, beating well after each addition. Add crab meat and stir over the heat until the mixture is hot and thickens again (do not let it boil). Pour into a large heatproof bowl, then add cayenne pepper and season.

Whisk the egg whites in a clean dry bowl until they form soft peaks. Spoon a quarter of the egg white onto the soufflé mixture and quickly but lightly fold it in, to loosen the mixture. Lightly fold in the remaining egg white. Put the ramekins on a baking tray. Spoon the mixture into the ramekins and then run your thumb around the inside rim of each ramekin. This ridge helps the soufflés to rise evenly without sticking.

Bake for 12–15 minutes, or until the soufflés are well risen and wobble slightly when tapped. Test with a skewer through a crack in the side of a soufflé; the skewer should come out clean or slightly moist. If the skewer is slightly moist, by the time the soufflés make it to the table they will be cooked in the centre. Serve immediately.

Once boiling, remove from heat then stand so flavours can infuse.

Put the ramekins on a tray then gently spoon in the mixture.

Poulpe provençal

Tender and sweet, fresh baby octopus are delectable when combined in a stew with tomatoes, wine and herbs. Some cooks have an aversion to dealing with octopus in its raw state, but they are simple to clean. Serve this dish with plenty of crusty baguette to mop up the tasty juices.

tomatoes	500 g (1 lb 2 oz) ripe
baby octopus	1 kg (2 lb 4 oz)
olive oil	3 tablespoons
onion	1 large, chopped
garlic	2 cloves
dry white wine	350 ml (11 fl oz/1⅓ cups)
saffron threads	¼ teaspoon
thyme	2 sprigs
flat-leaf (Italian) parsley	2 tablespoons, roughly chopped

Score a cross in the base of each tomato. Place tomatoes into boiling water for 20 seconds, then plunge into cold water and peel the skin away from the cross. Cut each tomato in half and scoop out seeds with a teaspoon and discard. Chop the flesh.

To clean the octopus, use a small sharp knife and cut each head from the tentacles. Remove eyes by cutting a round of flesh from the base of each head. To clean the heads, carefully slit them open and remove gut. Rinse thoroughly. Cut heads in half. Push out the beaks from the centre of the tentacles from the cut side. Cut the tentacles into sets of four or two, depending on the size of the octopus.

Blanch all the octopus in boiling water for 2 minutes, then drain and allow to cool slightly. Pat dry with paper towels.

Heat the olive oil in a saucepan, add the onion and cook for 7–8 minutes over medium heat until lightly golden. Add the octopus and the garlic to the pan and cook for a further 2–3 minutes. Add the tomato, wine, saffron and thyme. Add just enough water to cover the octopus.

Simmer, covered, for 1 hour. Uncover and cook for a further 15 minutes, or until the octopus is tender and the sauce has thickened a little. Season to taste. Serve sprinkled with parsley.

Cut the cleaned octopus heads and tentacles into halves.

Stir the tomato, wine, saffron and thyme into the octopus.

Garlic prawns

This is a universally popular dish and one that pops up often in the cuisine of Mediterranean countries. Here, the prawns are baked in the garlicky butter, rather than pan-fried, which makes the cooking easier. Choose the freshest, plumpest prawns you can find.

raw prawns (shrimp)	24 large
garlic	6 cloves, crushed
red chillies	1–2 small, very finely chopped
olive oil	250 ml (9 fl oz/1 cup)
butter	60 g (2¼ oz)
flat-leaf (Italian) parsley	2 tablespoons, chopped

Peel and devein the prawns, leaving the tails intact. Preheat the oven to 220°C (425°F/Gas 7). Sprinkle the garlic and chilli into four gratin dishes. Divide the oil and butter among the dishes.

Put the dishes on a baking tray in the oven and heat for about 6 minutes, or until the butter has melted.

Divide the prawns among the dishes. Bake for about 7 minutes, or until the prawns are pink and tender. Sprinkle with parsley. Serve immediately.

There are about 300 varieties of garlic, the most familiar sort having papery-white skin surrounding the tightly-packed cloves, although some types have reddish or purple skins. Seek out bulbs that are plump, smooth and firm. Garlic contains a volatile substance called allicin which is responsible for its aggressive smell and lingering aftertaste when eaten raw. This dissipates upon cooking, however, which is why large quantities of garlic can be used in a recipe without being overpowering. Garlic is highly prone to oxidation, which causes it to taste sharp and bitter, so avoid preparing it until just before you require it.

the perfect crêpes

Crêpes are simple and quick to make and versatile, lending themselves to both sweet and savoury dishes. Undeniably, there is a knack to making perfect crêpes — much of the secret lies in having a shallow, non-stick crêpe pan. Expect the first crêpes of any batch to be less than perfect; your pan should be hot so that as you add just enough batter to cover the base, it starts cooking straightaway. Some delicious fillings include sautéed mushrooms with ham, gruyère cheese and a dash of cream (whipping); steamed spinach with crème fraîche, grated nutmeg and grated lemon zest; and pitted cherries sautéed with butter and sprinkled with sugar, then flamed with brandy.

To make about 12 crêpes, sift 250 g (9 oz/2 cups) plain (all-purpose) flour, 1 teaspoon of sugar and a pinch of salt into a bowl then make a well in centre. In another bowl, whisk 2 eggs, then add 420 ml (14½ fl oz/1⅔ cups) milk and 4 tablespoons of water and whisk to combine. Slowly pour this mixture into the well, whisking to incorporate the flour, until a smooth batter forms. Stir in 1 tablespoon of melted butter, then cover and refrigerate for 20 minutes. Heat a crêpe pan and grease with butter. Pour in enough batter to thinly coat the base of the pan, swirling to coat, and pour out any excess. Cook over medium heat for 1 minute, or until the crêpe starts to come away from the side of pan, then turn over and cook for a further 1 minute or until golden. Stack the crêpes on a plate, alternating with pieces of baking paper. Cover with foil and keep warm in a 100°C (200°F/Gas ½) oven while cooking the remaining crêpes.

Moules marinière

Once you have mastered the technique of steaming mussels it's easy to whip up variations on this recipe. Add saffron and cream to the marinière mixture and you'll have mouclade; add chopped garlic, a bay leaf and some chopped tomatoes and it becomes moules à la provençal.

black mussels	26
onions	3, chopped
celery	1 stalk, chopped
white wine	250 ml (9 fl oz/1 cup)
fish stock	375 ml (13 fl oz/1½ cups)
flat-leaf (Italian) parsley	4 sprigs
thyme	1 sprig
bay leaf	1
butter	60 g (2¼ oz)
garlic	2 cloves, crushed
plain (all-purpose) flour	1 teaspoon
dill	sprigs, for serving

Scrub the mussels with a stiff brush and pull out the hairy beards. Discard any broken mussels, or open ones that don't close when tapped on the bench. Rinse well.

Put mussels, 1 onion, the celery and wine in a large saucepan and bring rapidly to the boil. Cover and cook, shaking the pan frequently, for 3 minutes. Remove mussels as they open. Discard any mussels that have not opened after 4–5 minutes.

Pull off and discard the empty side of each shell. Set aside the mussels in the shells, cover and keep warm. Strain and reserve the cooking liquid, discarding the vegetables.

In a saucepan, heat the fish stock, parsley, thyme and bay leaf. Bring to the boil, then reduce the heat. Cover and simmer for 1o minutes. Remove the herbs.

Melt the butter in a large saucepan and add the garlic and remaining onion. Stir over low heat for 5–1o minutes, or until the onion is soft but not brown. Stir in the flour and cook for 1 minute, or until pale and foaming. Remove from heat and gradually stir in the reserved mussel liquid and fish stock. Return to the heat and stir until mixture boils and thickens. Reduce the heat and simmer, uncovered, for 1o minutes.

Divide reserved mussels among four soup bowls. Ladle liquid over mussels and garnish with dill sprigs. Serve immediately.

Petits farcis

SERVES 4

Provence, the much-loved region that hugs the Mediterranean coastline in the French south, produces an abundance of vegetables and therefore an abundance of vegetable recipes. This one just needs crusty bread and some wine to provide an excellent light dinner or summer lunch.

eggplant (aubergines)	2 small, halved lengthways
zucchini (courgettes)	2 small, halved lengthways
tomatoes	4
red capsicum (peppers)	2 small, halved lengthways and seeded
olive oil	4 tablespoons
red onions	2, chopped
garlic	2 cloves, crushed
minced (ground) pork	250 g (9 oz)
minced (ground) veal	250 g (9 oz)
tomato paste (concentrated purée)	50 g (1¾ oz)
white wine	4 tablespoons
flat-leaf (Italian) parsley	2 tablespoons, chopped
parmesan cheese	50 g (1¾ oz), grated
fresh breadcrumbs	80 g (2¾ oz)

Preheat the oven to 180°C (350°F/Gas 4). Grease a roasting tin with oil. Use a spoon to hollow out the centres of the eggplant and zucchini, leaving a border around the edge. Chop the flesh.

Cut the tops from the tomatoes and reserve. Use a spoon to hollow out centres, catching the juice in a bowl, and chop the flesh roughly. Arrange the vegetables, including the capsicum, in the roasting tin. Brush the eggplant and zucchini with a little of the oil. Pour 125 ml (4½ fl oz/½ cup) of water into the roasting tin.

Heat half the oil in a large frying pan. Cook onion and garlic for 3 minutes, or until they have softened. Add the pork and veal and stir for 5 minutes, or until meat browns, breaking up any lumps with the back of a fork. Add chopped eggplant and zucchini and cook for a further 3 minutes. Add tomato pulp and juice, tomato paste and wine. Cook, stirring occasionally, for 10 minutes.

Remove the frying pan from the heat and stir in the parsley, parmesan and breadcrumbs. Season well with salt and pepper. Spoon the mixture into the vegetables. Place the tops back on the tomatoes. Sprinkle the vegetables with the remaining oil and bake for 45 minutes, or until the vegetables are tender.

Leave a border when hollowing out vegetables and brush with oil.

Use a fork to break up any lumps in the minced meat mixture.

Spoon the stuffing into the vegetables, keeping edges clean.

Zucchini omelette

Although an omelette is a very straightforward dish, eggs do require a gentle hand as they toughen if over-beaten or worked too much. The French favour a creamy-centred omelette and achieve this by cooking them on one side only.

butter	80 g (2¾ oz)
zucchini (courgettes)	400 g (14 oz), sliced
basil	1 tablespoon finely chopped
ground nutmeg	pinch
eggs	8, lightly beaten

Melt half the butter in a non-stick 23 cm (9 inch) frying pan. Add the zucchini and cook over medium heat for 8 minutes, or until lightly golden. Stir in the basil and nutmeg, season with salt and pepper and cook for 30 seconds. Transfer to a bowl and keep warm.

Wipe out the pan, return it to the heat and melt the remaining butter. Lightly season the eggs and pour into the pan. Stir gently over high heat. Stop stirring when the mixture begins to set in uniform, fluffy small clumps. Reduce the heat and lift the edges with a fork to prevent it catching. Shake the pan from side to side to prevent the omelette sticking. When it is almost set but still runny on the surface, spread the zucchini down the centre. Using a spatula, fold the omelette over and slide onto a serving plate.

Related to pumpkins (winter squash) and squash, zucchini ('courgette' in French and also called this in England) are a type of marrow picked when very small. These are at their best over spring, summer and autumn months. Choose zucchini that have glossy skins which show no trace of cuts, splits or bruising. The skin should be very tender (you should be able to pierce it with a fingernail). Choose the smallest zucchini on offer — these will have the sweetest flavour. Larger ones can be bland and full of seeds. Avoid refrigerating zucchini if possible as this adversely affects their texture but if unavoidable, use a vegetable storage bag and refrigerate for up to three days.

Many French main-course dishes involve time-honoured, classic pairings — chicken with tarragon, duck with orange, pork with prunes, quail with grapes, steak with red-wine sauce or fish with capers and fennel, for example. Most have evolved thanks to the traditional proximity of French cooks to the agricultural sources of their food; meats, aromatics and wines were combined because they happened to be both compatible as well as extremely handy. Even today, with supermarkets making more products available for longer seasons, and to larger spreads of people, the French do not feel the need, on the whole, to tinker with such enduring combinations.

Sauces are a striking feature of French cuisine and these are widely used to provide complementary flavours and textures for fish, meat or poultry. While some sauces rely on the cook having a good, home-made stock at hand (and stocks can easily be made in quantity and frozen in small portions, for convenience), many are quick, made-in-the-pan affairs, calling for reduced cream, cooking juices, a splash or two of wine or a few cubes of butter, to provide flavour, body and texture. Sauces add a touch of finesse to say, a simple steak (as with entrecôte à la bordelaise) a straightforward chicken sauté (poulet Vallée d'Auge, for example) and even a rabbit braise, where the cooking liquid is thickened and enriched with egg yolks and cream, thus defining it as a fricassee. The dishes included in this selection are not the notoriously complex ones of French haute cuisine, with their intricate and lengthy preparation, but rather ones more typical of home-style cooking.

It is from the French kitchen that we get the various, and basic, cooking techniques we employ in our own kitchens practically everyday. While other cuisines use braising, pot-roasting, shallow-frying, poaching, roasting and sautéing as methods of cooking too, it is surely in French versions that these are seen in their most polished form. Classic dishes like coq au vin and beef bourguignon, for example, demonstrate perfectly the depth of flavour and degree of tenderness that long, slow, moist cooking with herbs, wine and vegetables can achieve. A rack of lamb, roasted to medium–rare perfection gets, in French hands, further refinement from a simple herb crust and the 'Frenched', or scraped-clean, bones. Gentle poaching of seafood results in a seductive and sophisticated dish, yet one that is simplicity itself to execute. The cooking techniques used here are all straightforward — even novice cooks can approach these recipes with confidence.

Bouillabaisse

Many French regions have their own version of fish soup, or fish stew — this one, from the southern port city of Marseilles, is surely the most famous. Bouillabaisse is a great dish to cook for a crowd; its success lies in including a variety of fish and seafood.

rouille

red capsicum (pepper)	1 small
white bread	1 slice, crusts removed
red chilli	1
garlic	2 cloves
egg yolk	1
olive oil	4 tablespoons

soup

mussels	18
firm white fish fillets such as red mullet, bass, snapper, or John Dory	1.5 kg (3 lb 5 oz), skin on
oil	2 tablespoons
fennel bulb	1, thinly sliced
onion	1, chopped
tomatoes	750 g (1 lb 1o oz) ripe
fish stock or water	1.25 litres (44 fl oz/5 cups)
saffron threads	pinch
bouquet garni	1
orange zest	5 cm (2 in) piece

To make the rouille, preheat the grill (broiler). Cut the capsicum in half, remove the seeds and membrane and place, skin side up, under the hot grill until the skin blackens and blisters. Leave to cool before peeling away the skin. Roughly chop the capsicum.

Soak bread in 3 tablespoons of water, then squeeze dry with your hands. Put capsicum, bread, chilli, garlic and egg yolk in a mortar and pestle or food processor and pound or process together. Gradually add the oil in a thin stream, pounding or processing until the rouille is smooth and has the texture of thick mayonnaise. Cover and refrigerate until needed.

To make the soup, scrub the mussels with a stiff brush and pull out the hairy beards. Discard any broken mussels, or open ones that don't close when tapped on the bench. Rinse well. Cut the fish into bite-sized pieces.

Heat the oil in a large saucepan and cook the fennel and onion over medium heat for 5 minutes, or until golden.

Score a cross in the base of each tomato. Plunge into boiling water for 20 seconds, then drain and peel the skin away from the cross. Chop the tomatoes, discarding the cores. Add to the pan and cook for 3 minutes. Stir in the stock, saffron, bouquet garni and orange zest, bring to the boil and boil for 1o minutes. Remove the bouquet garni and either push the soup through a sieve or purée in a blender. Return to the cleaned pan, season well and bring back to the boil.

Reduce the heat and add the fish and mussels. Cook for 5 minutes, or until the fish is tender and the mussels have opened. Discard any mussels that haven't opened. Serve the soup with rouille and bread.

Soften the fennel and onion then add the remaining ingredients.

Push vegetables through a sieve then discard remaining solids.

Poached seafood with herb aïoli

The southern French are addicted to aïoli, to the extent that this lush, super-garlicky mayonnaise is often called the 'butter of Provence'. Poaching is one of the gentlest ways to cook seafood and, as it uses no fat, is an ideal method when pairing fish with oil-rich aïoli.

raw lobster tails	2
mussels	12
scallops	250 g (9 oz) on their shells
raw prawns (shrimp)	500 g (1 lb 2 oz)
dry white wine	250 ml (9 fl oz/1 cup)
fish stock	250 ml (9 fl oz/1 cup)
saffron threads	pinch
bay leaf	1
black peppercorns	4
salmon fillets	4 x 50 g (1¾ oz)

herb aïoli

egg yolks	4
garlic	4 cloves, crushed
basil	1 tablespoon, chopped
flat-leaf (Italian) parsley	4 tablespoons, chopped
lemon juice	1 tablespoon
olive oil	200 ml (7 fl oz)
lemon wedges	to serve

Remove the lobster meat from the tail by cutting down each side of the underside with scissors and peeling back the middle piece of shell. Scrub the mussels with a stiff brush and pull out the hairy beards. Discard any broken mussels, or open ones that don't close when tapped on the bench. Rinse well. Remove the scallops from their shells and pull away the white muscle and digestive tract around each one, leaving the roes intact. Clean the scallop shells and keep them for serving. Peel and devein the prawns, leaving the tails intact; butterfly prawns by cutting them open down the backs.

To make the herb aïoli, put the egg yolks, garlic, basil, parsley and lemon juice in a mortar and pestle or food processor and pound or process until light and creamy. Add the oil, drop by drop from the tip of a teaspoon, pounding or processing constantly until the mixture begins to thicken, then add the oil in a very thin stream.

Put the wine, stock, saffron, bay leaf and peppercorns in a frying pan and bring to a very slow simmer. Add the lobster and poach for 5 minutes then remove, cover and keep warm. Poach the remaining seafood in batches — the mussels and scallops will take about 2 minutes to cook (discard any mussels that have not opened). The prawns will take 3 minutes and the salmon a little longer, depending on the thickness. Cut the lobster into thick slices, put the scallops back on their shells and arrange the seafood on a large platter with the aïoli in a bowl in the centre. Serve with lemon wedges.

Boeuf à la ficelle

Beef fillet — a lean, tender cut — is normally grilled, pan-fried or roasted. In this classic preparation it is poached in beef stock. The name translates as 'beef on a string', in reference to the kitchen string used to tie the beef, lower it into the stock then raise it when cooked.

centre-cut beef fillet	800 g (1 lb 12 oz)
beef stock	900 ml (31 fl oz)
swede (rutabaga)	1, cut into batons
carrot	1, cut into batons
celery	1 stalk, cut into batons
all-purpose potatoes	2, cut into chunks
cabbage	¼, chopped
spring onions (scallions)	4, trimmed into long lengths
bay leaf	1
thyme sprigs	2
flat-leaf (Italian) parsley sprigs	2

Trim beef of any fat and sinew and cut into four even pieces. Tie each piece of beef around its circumference with kitchen string so it keeps its compact shape. Leave a long length of string attached, to lower the beef in and out of the stock.

Put stock in a saucepan, bring to the boil and add vegetables and herbs. Cook over medium heat for about 8 minutes, or until the vegetables are tender. Lift out the vegetables with a slotted spoon and keep warm. Discard the herbs and skim the stock of any foam that floats to the surface.

Season beef with salt, then lower into the simmering stock, keeping the strings tied around the saucepan handle or a wooden spoon balanced over pan. Cook for about 6 minutes for rare, or 10 minutes for medium–rare, depending on your taste.

Place each piece of beef in a large shallow bowl and loop the end of the string onto the rim of the bowl. Add the cooked vegetables and ladle some of the cooking broth over the top to serve.

Swedes (rutabagas) have an undeservedly bad reputation, possibly as a result of bad cooking practices. They possess, though, an earthy sweetness that is quite delicious and one that is perfectly complementary to the deep, savoury flavours of this poached beef dish. The result of a seventeenth century cross between the turnip and the cabbage, swedes are a cold climate vegetable and are at their best during the winter months. Choose swedes that are heavy for their size. Swedes are a long-keeping vegetable and are often sold with a wax coating — in any case they need peeling before using and, if the layer under the skin is fibrous, pare this away too.

Lobster thermidor

SERVES 4

This dish was first served in Paris in 1894 on the opening night of a play called 'Thermidor', after which it was named. Thermidor, which translates from the Greek as 'gift of heat', was originally the name of the eleventh month of the French Republican calendar, in use between 1793 and 1805.

lobsters	2, live
fish stock	250 ml (9 fl oz/1 cup)
white wine	2 tablespoons
French shallots	2, finely chopped
chervil	2 teaspoons, chopped
tarragon	2 teaspoons, chopped
butter	110 g (3¾ oz)
plain (all-purpose) flour	2 tablespoons
dry mustard	1 teaspoon
milk	250 ml (9 fl oz/1 cup)
parmesan cheese	60 g (2¼ oz), grated

Put the lobsters in freezer for 1 hour before you want to cook them. Bring a large saucepan of water to the boil, add lobsters and cook for 10 minutes. Drain and cool slightly before cutting off heads. Cut the lobster tails in half lengthways and remove digestive tract. Use a spoon to ease meat out of shells and cut into bite-sized pieces. Rinse shells, pat dry and keep for serving.

Put the stock, wine, shallot, chervil and tarragon into a small saucepan. Boil until reduced by half, then strain.

Melt 60 g (2¼ oz) of the butter in a heavy-based saucepan and stir in the flour and mustard to make a roux. Cook, stirring, for 2 minutes over low heat without allowing the roux to brown.

Remove from heat and add milk and reserved stock mixture gradually, stirring after each addition until smooth. Return to the heat and stir until the sauce boils and thickens. Simmer, stirring, for 3 minutes. Stir in half the parmesan and season.

Heat remaining butter in a frying pan and fry the lobster over medium heat for 2 minutes, or until lightly browned — take care not to overcook. Preheat the grill (broiler). Divide half the sauce among lobster shells, top with lobster meat and then finish with the remaining sauce. Sprinkle with the remaining parmesan and place under the grill until golden brown.

Ease lobster meat out of the shell in once piece using a spoon.

Stir the liquid gradually into the roux so lumps don't form.

Use two spoons to drop sauce over the lobster meat in shells.

Chicken with forty cloves of garlic

SERVES 4

Forty cloves of garlic might sound excessive but here, the garlic cooks into a nutty, sweet and mild-flavoured pulp that is wonderful with the chicken. Serve the dish with buttered noodles or rice to soak up all the flavoursome juices.

celery	2 stalks, including leaves
rosemary	2 sprigs, plus extra to garnish
thyme	4 sprigs, plus extra to garnish
flat-leaf (Italian) parsley	4 sprigs, plus extra to garnish
whole chicken	1.6 kg (3 lb 8 oz)
garlic	40 cloves, unpeeled
olive oil	2 tablespoons
carrot	1, roughly chopped
onion	1 small, cut into 4 wedges
white wine	250 ml (9 fl oz/1 cup)
baguette	1, cut into slices

Preheat the oven to 200°C (400°F/Gas 6). Put a chopped celery stalk and 2 sprigs each of the rosemary, thyme and parsley into the chicken cavity. Add 6 garlic cloves. Tie the legs together and tuck the wing tips under.

Brush the chicken liberally with some of the oil and season well. Scatter about 10 more garlic cloves in a large saucepan. Put the remaining sprigs of herbs, chopped celery, carrot and onion in the saucepan.

Put the chicken into the saucepan. Scatter remaining garlic cloves around the chicken and add the remaining oil and the wine. Cover and bake for 1 hour 20 minutes, or until the chicken is tender and the juices run clear when the thigh is pierced with a skewer.

To serve, carefully lift the chicken out of the saucepan. Drain the juices into a small saucepan. Remove the garlic cloves from the drained mixture and set aside. Spoon off the fat from the juices and boil for 2–3 minutes to reduce and thicken a little.

Cut the chicken into serving portions, pour over a little of the juices and scatter with the garlic. Toast the baguette slices, then spread with the soft flesh squeezed from the garlic. Garnish the chicken with herb sprigs and serve with the baguette slices.

Use kitchen string to securely tie the chicken legs together.

Pour the wine and remaining oil over the chicken.

Duck a l'orange

SERVES 4

This brilliant combination, where sharp, sweet citrus juices cut through the richness of duck and complement its meaty flavours, dates from the 17th century. The French aren't particularly fond of sweet/savoury combinations, so this delicious dish is a little unusual.

oranges	5
whole duck	2 kg (4 lb 8 oz)
cinnamon	2 sticks
mint	1 large handful
soft brown sugar	95 g (3¼ oz)
cider vinegar	125 ml (4 fl oz/½ cup)
Grand Marnier	80 ml (2½ fl oz/⅓ cup)
butter	30 g (1 oz)

Preheat oven to 150°C (300°F/Gas 2). Halve two of the oranges and rub all over the duck. Place them inside the duck cavity with cinnamon sticks and mint. Tie the legs together and tie the wings together. Prick the skin all over with a carving fork.

Put duck on a rack, breast side down, and put rack in a shallow roasting tin. Roast for 45 minutes, turning halfway through.

Meanwhile, zest and juice remaining oranges. Heat sugar in a saucepan over low heat until it melts and caramelizes: swirl pan to make sure it caramelizes evenly. When sugar is a rich brown, add vinegar and boil for 3 minutes. Add orange juice and Grand Marnier and simmer for 2 minutes. Blanch orange zest in boiling water for 1 minute three times, changing water each time. Refresh under cold water, then drain and reserve.

Remove excess fat from roasting tin. Increase the oven to 180°C (350°F/Gas 4). Spoon some of the orange sauce over the duck. Roast for 45 minutes, spooning the remaining sauce over the duck every 10 minutes and turning the duck to baste all sides.

Remove duck from oven, cover with foil and strain juices back into a saucepan. Skim off any excess fat and add orange zest and butter to the saucepan. Stir to melt butter. Reheat sauce and serve over the duck.

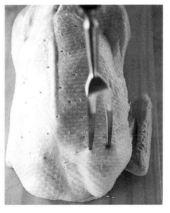

Prick skin with a carving fork to release excess fat during cooking.

A citrus zester makes easy work of cutting zest into fine strips.

Pork chops with braised red cabbage

This dish may not sound overly French but remember that Alsace and Lorraine border on Germany, where this treatment of cabbage is typical. Even sworn non-cabbage lovers will warm to this slightly sweet dish, which you could also serve with roast pork or pork fillet, if you preferred.

braised red cabbage

clarified butter	30 g (1 oz)
onion	1, finely chopped
garlic	1 clove, crushed
red cabbage	1 small, shredded
cooking apple	1, peeled, cored and finely sliced
red wine	4 tablespoons
red wine vinegar	1 tablespoon
ground cloves	¼ teaspoon
sage	1 tablespoon, finely chopped
clarified butter	15 g (½ oz)
pork chops	4 x 200 g (7 oz), trimmed
white wine	4 tablespoons
chicken stock	400 ml (14 fl oz)
thick (double/heavy) cream	3 tablespoons
dijon mustard	1½ tablespoons
sage leaves	4

To braise the cabbage, put the clarified butter in a saucepan, add onion and garlic and cook until softened but not browned. Add cabbage, apple, wine, vinegar, cloves and sage and season with salt and pepper. Cover pan and cook for 30 minutes over low heat. Uncover the pan and then cook, stirring, for a further 5 minutes to evaporate any liquid.

Meanwhile, heat the clarified butter in a frying pan, season the chops and brown well on both sides. Add the wine and stock. Cover and simmer for 20 minutes, or until the pork is tender.

Remove chops from the frying pan and strain the liquid. Return the liquid to the pan, bring to the boil and cook until reduced by two-thirds. Add the cream and mustard and stir over very low heat without allowing to boil, until sauce has thickened slightly. Pour sauce over the pork chops and garnish with sage. Serve with the red cabbage.

Cabbages come in a variety of shapes, sizes and colours but surely none can be more alluring than the red sort. Red, or purple, cabbage has long been associated with Eastern European and German cooking and, with its tough leaves and thick central veins, it is ideally suited to braising and other methods of long cooking. The compound which gives this cabbage its gorgeous colour is called anthocyanin and, when cooked with alkaline ingredients, it reacts and turns the cabbage blue. Introducing an acid element (a teaspoon of vinegar or lemon juice, for example) will help preserve the red colour and can even restore it.

Roast duck with olives

Here's an inspired main course — succulent, crisp-skinned duck with a light, rice-based stuffing and a thick tomato and olive sauce. For optimum results, buy a fresh duck from a good supplier — if going to the trouble to cook such a bird, you should get your hands on the best one you can.

sauce

olive oil	1 tablespoon
onion	1, chopped
garlic	1 clove, crushed
roma (plum) tomatoes	2 ripe, peeled and chopped
riesling	250 ml (9 fl oz/1 cup)
thyme	2 teaspoons
bay leaf	1
niçoise olives	24, pitted

stuffing

medium-grain rice	60 g (2¼ oz/⅓ cup), cooked
garlic	1 clove, crushed
English spinach	100 g (3½ oz) frozen chopped, defrosted
duck's livers	2, chopped
egg	1, lightly beaten
thyme	1 teaspoon
duck	1.8 kg (4 lb)
bay leaves	2

Preheat the oven to 200°C (400°F/Gas 6). To make the sauce, heat oil in a frying pan, add the onion and cook for 5 minutes, or until transparent. Add garlic, tomato, wine and herbs and season well. Cook for 5 minutes, then add the olives before removing from the heat.

To make stuffing, thoroughly mix all the ingredients in a bowl and season well. Before stuffing the duck, rinse out the cavity with cold water and pat dry inside and out with paper towels. Put the bay leaves in the cavity, then spoon in the stuffing.

Tuck the wings under the duck, then close the flaps of skin over the parson's nose and secure with a skewer or toothpick. Place in a deep baking dish and rub 1 teaspoon salt into the skin. Prick the skin all over with a carving fork.

Roast on the top shelf for 35–40 minutes, then carefully pour off the excess fat. Roast for another 35–40 minutes. To check that the duck is cooked, gently pull away one leg from the side. The flesh should be pale brown with no blood in the juices. Remove, then carve, serving a spoonful of the stuffing next to the duck and topping with the sauce.

Use a spoon to pack the stuffing into the duck cavity.

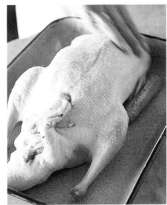

Tuck wings under the duck and use toothpicks to close the cavity.

three ways with fish

For optimum eating enjoyment, the freshest of fish just needs very straightforward preparation and cooking. The French, particularly those from coastal regions such as the Mediterranean areas of Provence, excel in un-fussy approaches to fish cookery. Baking fish in a paper packet, for example, ensures that no precious juices are lost and also locks in the aromatic flavours of leek and lemon. There are few more satisfying (or simple) ways to prepare fish than sautéeing it in butter, which basically describes sole meunière — use fillets instead of whole fish here if you prefer.

GRILLED RED MULLET WITH HERB SAUCE

Preheat a barbecue grill plate or chargrill pan. Make a couple of deep slashes in the thickest part of each 4 x 200 g (7 oz) red mullet. Pat the fish dry and sprinkle inside and out with salt and pepper. Drizzle with 3 tablespoons lemon juice and 3 tablespoons olive oil and cook on the barbecue for 4–5 minutes each side, or until the fish flakes when tested with the tip of a knife. Baste with lemon juice and oil during cooking. To make the sauce, wash 100 g (3^1/$_2$ oz) English spinach leaves and put in a large saucepan with just the water clinging to the leaves. Cover the pan and steam the spinach for 2 minutes, or until just wilted. Drain, cool and squeeze with your hands to get rid of the excess liquid. Finely chop. Put 3 tablespoons olive oil, 1 tablespoon white wine vinegar, 1 tablespoon chopped flat-leaf (Italian) parsley, 1 tablespoon chopped chives, 1 tablespoon chopped chervil, 1 tablespoon finely chopped capers, 2 finely chopped anchovy fillets, 1 finely chopped hard-boiled egg and the spinach in a mortar and pestle or food processor and pound or process until smooth. Spoon the sauce onto a plate and place the fish on top to serve. Serves 4.

FISH COOKED IN PAPER

Preheat the oven to 180°C (350°F/Gas 4). Place each of 4 skinless fish fillets (200 g/7 oz each), such as snapper, in the centre of a piece of baking paper large enough to enclose the fish. Season lightly. Scatter with 1 leek, white part only, julienned, and 4 spring onions (scallions), julienned. Top each with 5 g (1/$_8$ oz) butter. Cut 1 lemon into 12 very thin slices and top each piece of fish with 3 lemon slices. Sprinkle with 2–3 tablespoons lemon juice. Bring the paper together and fold over several times. Fold the ends under. Bake on a baking tray for 20 minutes (the steam will make the paper puff up). Check to see that the fish is cooked (it should be white and flake easily when tested with a fork) and then serve. Serve as parcels or lift the fish out and pour the juices over. Serves 4.

SOLE MEUNIÈRE

Using paper towels, pat-dry 4 whole sole, gutted and dark skin removed, cutting off the heads if you prefer. Dust lightly with 3 tablespoons plain (all-purpose) flour and season. Heat 150 g (5^1/$_2$ oz) butter in a frying pan large enough to fit all four fish, or use half the butter and cook the fish in two batches. Put the fish in the pan, skin side up, and cook for 4 minutes on each side or until golden. Lift the fish out onto warm plates and drizzle with 2 tablespoons lemon juice and 4 tablespoons chopped flat-leaf (Italian) parsley. Add 50 g (1^3/$_4$ oz) butter to the pan and heat until it browns to make a beurre noisette (brown butter). Pour over the fish (it will foam as it mixes with the lemon juice) and serve with lemon wedges. Serves 4.

grilled red mullet with herb sauce

Gasconnade

SERVES 6

This recipe uses quantities of soft, cooked garlic to great effect — here it is puréed then combined with stock to form a sauce. Aromatic herbs and anchovies flavour the cooked lamb, which should be well rested before carving; this allows all the juices to settle into the meat.

leg of lamb	1 large, about 2.5 kg (5 lb), partially boned
carrot	1, coarsely chopped
celery	1 stalk, coarsely chopped
onion	1 large, coarsely chopped
bay leaf	1
bouquet garni	1
garlic	2 cloves, crushed
anchovy fillets	6, mashed
flat-leaf (Italian) parsley	2 teaspoons, finely chopped
thyme	2 teaspoons, finely chopped
rosemary	2 teaspoons, finely chopped
olive oil	3 tablespoons
garlic	25 cloves, unpeeled

Preheat the oven to 220°C (425°F/Gas 7). Place the removed lamb bone in a stockpot with the carrot, celery, onion, bay leaf and bouquet garni, and add just enough cold water to cover. Bring to the boil and simmer uncovered for 1 hour. Strain and if necessary simmer until reduced to 500 ml (17 fl oz/2 cups).

Meanwhile, combine the crushed garlic, anchovies, chopped herbs and olive oil in a small bowl with some freshly ground black pepper. Rub the cavity of the lamb with most of the herb mixture. Roll the meat up and tie securely with kitchen string. Rub the outside of the lamb with the remaining herb mixture and place in a flameproof baking dish. Bake for 15 minutes, then reduce the temperature to 180°C (350°F/Gas 4). Continue baking for about 45 minutes (for medium–rare), basting with the pan juices occasionally, or until cooked to your liking.

Bring a saucepan of water to the boil and add the unpeeled garlic cloves. Boil for 5 minutes. Drain and rinse under cold water. Peel the garlic and purée the pulp. Put it in the saucepan with the 500 ml (17 fl oz/2 cups) of stock and bring to the boil. Simmer for 10 minutes. Transfer the lamb to a carving board and keep warm. Spoon off the fat from the pan juices in a dish. Add the garlic stock and place the dish over high heat. Bring to the boil and cook until reduced by half. Adjust the seasoning. Serve the lamb sliced, accompanied by the sauce.

Lay the lamb out flat and spread with the anchovy mixture.

Roll the lamb and tie it at regular intervals with kitchen string.

Rack of lamb with herb crust

SERVES 4

Racks of lamb always look dramatic when presented at the table, especially if you buy ones that have been French trimmed. The herb crust here makes the racks look even more professional — this is a dish worthy of any smart restaurant but is actually very achievable at home.

racks of lamb	2 x 6-cutlet, trimmed and bones cleaned (ask your butcher to do this)
oil	1 tablespoon
fresh breadcrumbs	80 g (2¾ oz/1 cup)
garlic	3 cloves
flat-leaf (Italian) parsley	3 tablespoons, finely chopped
thyme	2 teaspoons
lemon zest	½ teaspoon, finely grated
butter	60 g (2¼ oz), softened
sauce	
beef stock	250 ml (9 fl oz/1 cup)
garlic	1 clove, finely chopped
thyme	1 sprig

Preheat the oven to 250°C (500°F/Gas 9). Score the fat on the racks in a diamond pattern. Rub the rack with a little of the oil and season with salt and pepper.

Heat the oil in a frying pan over high heat, add the lamb and brown for 4–5 minutes. Remove and set aside, reserving the pan for later.

In a large bowl, mix the breadcrumbs, garlic, parsley, thyme and lemon zest. Season, then mix in the butter to form a paste.

Firmly press a layer of breadcrumb mixture over the fat on the racks, leaving the bones and base clean. Bake in a baking dish for 12 minutes for medium–rare, or until cooked to your liking. Allow to rest.

To make the sauce, add the beef stock, extra garlic and thyme sprig to the roasting pan juices, scraping the pan. Return this liquid to the original frying pan and simmer over high heat for 5–8 minutes, until the sauce is reduced and thickened slightly. Strain and serve on the side.

Use a sharp knife to score the fat in a diamond pattern.

The crust is easily made, just mix ingredients together with a spoon.

Use a spoon, or wet hands, to press the crust over the lamb.

Boeuf bourguignon

This classic braise from Burgundy (famous for its red wine), benefits from being cooked a day in advance. By replacing the wine with dark beer, doubling the quantity of onions and leaving out the carrot, you have carbonnade, another classic French stew from up near the border with Belgium.

beef blade or chuck steak	1.5 kg (3 lb 5 oz)
red wine (preferably burgundy)	750 ml (26 fl oz/3 cups)
garlic	3 cloves, crushed
bouquet garni	1
butter	70 g (2½ oz)
onion	1, chopped
carrot	1, chopped
plain (all-purpose) flour	2 tablespoons
bacon slices	200 g (7 oz), cut into short strips
French shallots	300 g (10½ oz), peeled
button mushrooms	200 g (7 oz) small

Cut meat into 4 cm (1¼ in) cubes and trim away any excess fat. Put meat, wine, garlic and bouquet garni in a bowl, cover with plastic wrap and refrigerate for at least 3 hours, or overnight.

Preheat the oven to 160°C (315°F/Gas 2–3). Drain the meat, reserving the marinade and bouquet garni, and pat-dry on paper towels. Heat 30 g (1 oz) of the butter in a large casserole dish. Add onion, carrot and bouquet garni and cook over low heat, stirring occasionally, for 10 minutes. Remove from heat.

Heat 20 g (¾ oz) of the butter in a large frying pan over high heat. Fry the meat in batches for about 5 minutes, or until well browned. Add to the casserole dish.

Pour the reserved marinade into the frying pan and boil, stirring, for 30 seconds to deglaze the pan. Remove from the heat. Return the casserole to high heat and sprinkle the meat and vegetables with the flour. Cook, stirring constantly, until the meat is well coated with the flour. Pour in the marinade and stir well. Bring to the boil, stirring constantly, then cover and cook in the oven for 2 hours.

Heat the remaining butter in the clean frying pan and cook the bacon and shallots, stirring, for 8–10 minutes or until the shallots are softened but not browned. Add the mushrooms and cook, stirring occasionally, for 2–3 minutes or until browned. Drain on paper towels. Add the shallots, bacon and mushrooms to the casserole.

Cover the casserole and return to the oven for 30 minutes, or until the meat is tender. Discard the bouquet garni. Skim any fat from the surface and season before serving.

Coq au vin

Meat (and fish, for that matter) cooked on the bone always has a far superior flavour than that cooked off the bone — it is worth honing the few skills required to cut a whole, fresh chicken into pieces just so you can make this satisfying dish.

whole chicken	2 x 1.6 kg (3 lb 8 oz)
red wine	750 ml (26 fl oz/3 cups)
bay leaves	2
thyme	2 sprigs
bacon slices	250 g (9 oz), diced
butter	60 g (2¼ oz)
baby onions	20
button mushrooms	250 g (9 oz)
oil	1 teaspoon
plain (all-purpose) flour	30 g (1 oz)
chicken stock	1 litre (35 fl oz/4 cups)
brandy	125 ml (4 fl oz/½ cup)
tomato paste (concentrated purée)	2 teaspoons
butter	30 g (1 oz), softened
plain (all-purpose) flour	1 tablespoon
flat-leaf (Italian) parsley	2 tablespoons, chopped

Joint each chicken into eight pieces by removing both legs and cutting between the joint of the drumstick and the thigh. Cut down either side of the backbone and lift it out. Turn the chicken over and cut through the cartilage down the centre of the breastbone. Cut each breast in half, leaving the wing attached to the top half.

Put the wine, bay leaves, thyme and some salt and pepper in a bowl and add chicken. Cover and then refrigerate for 4 hours, or overnight.

Blanch bacon in boiling water, then drain, pat dry and sauté in a frying pan until golden. Lift out onto a plate. Melt 15 g (½ oz) of the butter in the pan, add the onions and sauté until browned. Lift out and set aside.

Melt a further 15 g (½ oz) of the butter, add the mushrooms, season with salt and pepper and sauté for 5 minutes. Remove and set aside.

Drain the chicken, reserving the marinade, and pat the chicken dry. Season. Add the remaining butter and the oil to the frying pan, add the chicken and sauté until golden. Stir in the flour.

Transfer chicken to a large saucepan or casserole and add stock. Pour brandy into frying pan and boil, stirring, for 30 seconds to deglaze the pan. Pour over chicken. Add marinade, onions, mushrooms, bacon and tomato paste. Cook over medium heat for 45 minutes, or until chicken is cooked through.

If sauce needs thickening, lift out the chicken and vegetables and bring the sauce to the boil. Mix together the butter and the flour and whisk into the sauce. Boil, stirring, for 2 minutes or until thickened. Add parsley and return the chicken and vegetables to the sauce.

Marinating the chicken overnight gives it greater depth of flavour.

Cook chicken, turning, until the skin is deep golden.

Poulet vallée d'auge

SERVES 4

Normandy and Brittany are famous for their apples and cider. They are also famed for their peerless dairy products — many of the luscious dishes from these Northern Atlantic regions are decadently awash with cream and butter.

whole chicken	1.6 kg (3 lb 8 oz)
cooking apples	2
lemon juice	1 tablespoon
butter	60 g (2¼ oz)
onion	½, finely chopped
celery	½ stalk, finely chopped
plain (all-purpose) flour	2 teaspoons
Calvados or brandy	4 tablespoons
chicken stock	375 ml (13 fl oz/1½ cups)
crème fraîche	100 g (3½ oz)

Joint the chicken into eight pieces by removing both legs and cutting between the joint of the drumstick and the thigh. Cut down either side of the backbone and lift it out. Turn the chicken over and cut through the cartilage down the centre of the breastbone. Cut each breast in half, leaving the wing attached to the top half.

Peel and core the apples. Finely chop half of one apple and cut the rest into 12 wedges. Toss the apple in the lemon juice.

Heat half the butter in a large frying pan, then add the chicken pieces, skin side down, and cook until golden. Turn over and cook for a further 5 minutes. Lift the chicken out of the pan and tip away the fat.

Heat a further 20 g (¾ oz) of butter in the same pan and add the onion, celery and chopped apple. Fry over medium heat for 5 minutes without browning. Remove from the heat.

Sprinkle the flour over the vegetables and stir in. Add the Calvados and return to the heat. Gradually stir in the chicken stock. Bring to the boil, then return the chicken to the pan. Cover and simmer gently for 15 minutes, or until the chicken is tender and cooked through.

Meanwhile, heat the remaining butter in a small frying pan. Add the apple wedges and fry over medium heat until browned and tender. Remove from the pan and keep warm.

Remove the chicken from the pan and keep warm. Skim the excess fat from the cooking liquid. Add the crème fraîche. Bring to the boil and boil for 4 minutes, or until the sauce is thick enough to lightly coat the back of a wooden spoon. Season and pour over the chicken. Serve with the apple wedges.

Salt pork with lentils

The little slate-green puy lentils, from the Auvergne township of Le Puy-en-Velay, are prized the world over for their superior flavour. They are much more expensive than regular brown lentils (which you can use if you wish) but are well worth seeking out from specialty food stores.

salt pork belly	1 kg (2 lb 4 oz), cut into thick strips
salt pork knuckle	1 small
carrot	1 large, cut into chunks
swede (rutabaga) or turnip	200 g (7 oz), peeled and cut into chunks
leek	100 g (3½ oz), white part only, thickly sliced
parsnip	1, cut into chunks
onion	1, studded with 4 cloves
garlic	1 clove
bouquet garni	1
bay leaves	2
juniper berries	6, slightly crushed
Puy lentils	350 g (12 oz)
flat-leaf (Italian) parsley	2 tablespoons, chopped

Depending on the saltiness of the pork you are using, you may need to soak it in cold water for several hours or blanch it before using. Ask your butcher whether to do this.

Put pork in a large saucepan with all the ingredients except the lentils and parsley. Stir thoroughly, then add just enough water to cover the ingredients. Bring to the boil, then reduce the heat. Cover the pan and leave to simmer gently for 1¼ hours.

Put the lentils in a sieve and rinse under cold running water. Add to the saucepan and stir, then cover and simmer for a further 45–50 minutes, or until the pork and lentils are tender.

Drain the pan into a colander, discarding the liquid and white onion. Return the contents of the colander to the saucepan. Season to taste and stir in the parsley. Serve immediately.

A bouquet garni is a classic French seasoning, lending its sweet, herbal fragrance to all manner of stocks, soups, stews, sauces and braises. The most common components are dried or fresh bay leaves (the latter are quite strong so should be used sparingly), curly parsley stalks and sprigs of fresh thyme. These are tied together (kitchen string is fine for this) and simmered directly in the stock, then removed or strained out at the finish of cooking. The amounts of herbs used in the bundle vary according to the volumes of food being cooked and sage and strips of carrot and celery leaves can also be included, if desired.

Rabbit fricassee

SERVES 4

In France, you'd buy your wild rabbit from the market. In more supermarket-dominated societies, finding a wild rabbit is a tall order so farmed white rabbit will need to be substituted. Although flavour is not as pronounced, white rabbit does have the advantage of being meatier.

clarified butter	60 g (2¼ oz)
rabbit	1.5 kg (3 lb 5 oz), cut into 8 pieces
button mushrooms	200 g (7 oz)
white wine	100 ml (3½ fl oz)
chicken stock	150 ml (5 fl oz)
bouquet garni	1
oil	100 ml (3½ fl oz)
sage	40 g (1½ oz)
thick (double/heavy) cream	150 ml (5 fl oz)
egg yolks	2

Heat half the clarified butter in a large saucepan. Season the rabbit and brown in batches, turning once. Remove from the saucepan and set aside. Add the remaining butter to the saucepan and brown the mushrooms.

Put the rabbit back into the saucepan with the mushrooms. Add the wine and boil for a few minutes before adding the stock and bouquet garni. Cover and simmer gently over very low heat for 40 minutes.

Meanwhile, heat the oil in a small saucepan. Remove leaves from the sage and drop them, a few at a time, into the hot oil. Cook for 30 seconds, or until bright green and crisp. Drain the leaves on paper towels and sprinkle with salt.

Lift the cooked rabbit and mushrooms out of the saucepan and keep warm. Discard the bouquet garni. Remove pan from the heat, mix together the cream and egg yolks and whisk quickly into the stock. Return to very low heat and cook, whisking, for about 5 minutes or until thickened slightly (don't let the sauce boil or the yolks will scramble). Season with salt and pepper.

To serve, pour the sauce over the rabbit and mushrooms and garnish with crisp sage leaves.

Don't crowd the pan when browning the rabbit pieces.

Whisk the yolks and cream into the hot stock off the heat.

the perfect boeuf en croûte

This dish might be better known as Beef Wellington, but whatever it's called, beef en croûte makes for an impressive dinner party main course. In order for the meat to cook evenly, it is important it is the same thickness — either have your butcher prepare a piece of centre-cut fillet for you or tuck the thin end under the fillet before tying it, to give a piece that is approximately the same circumference all the way along. While this may look like a complicated dish to make, it is really straightforward.

Preheat the oven to 220°C (425°F/Gas 7). To make your own pâté, melt 90 g (3¼ oz) butter in a frying pan, then add 3 chopped French shallots and 1 chopped garlic clove. Stir over medium heat for a few minutes until softened. Add 360 g (12 oz) trimmed chicken livers and cook, stirring, for 4–5 minutes, or until cooked. Cool the livers, then combine with shallots, garlic, pan juices, 1 tablespoon brandy and remaining butter, in a food processor. Process until smooth and season.

Using kitchen string, tie a 1 kg (2 lb 4 oz) piece of trimmed beef fillet at 5 cm (2 in) intervals to form a neat shape. Heat 30 g (1 oz) butter in a roasting pan, add beef then brown all over. Place in the oven and cook for 20 minutes, then cool to room temperature and remove the string. Reduce the oven to 200°C (400°F/Gas 6). Roll 600 g (1 lb 5 oz) purchased block puff pastry into a 3 mm (⅛ in) thick rectangle large enough to enclose the beef, trim edges and reserve for decoration. Spread the pâté over the pastry, leaving a 1.5 cm (⅝ in) border then brush border with lightly beaten egg. Place the fillet on the pastry then use the pastry to wrap it tightly, pressing seams firmly to seal and tucking ends under. Place the package, seam side down, on a baking tray then brush all over with beaten egg. Cut shapes from the trimmings to decorate, then brush with egg. Bake for 25–30 minutes for rare and 35–40 minutes for medium. Stand boeuf en croûte for 5 minutes before slicing.

Lamb braised with beans

It has become so fashionable to serve lamb medium−rare that it is easy to forget how absolutely scrumptious it can be when cooked long and slow until the meat is almost fall-apart soft. Dried beans are also used here and the most convenient way to soak these is overnight in cold water.

dried haricot beans	125 g (4½ oz)
shoulder of lamb	1 kg (2 lb 4 oz) boned, tied with string to keep its shape
clarified butter	30 g (1 oz)
carrots	2, diced
onions	2 large, chopped
garlic	4 cloves, unpeeled
bouquet garni	1
dry red wine	250 ml (9 fl oz/1 cup)
beef stock	250 ml (9 fl oz/1 cup)

Put the beans in a large bowl and cover with plenty of water. Leave to soak for 8–12 hours, then drain. Bring a large saucepan of water to the boil, add beans and return to the boil. Reduce the heat to moderate and cook the beans, partially covered, for 40 minutes. Drain well.

Rub the lamb all over with salt and pepper. Heat the butter over high heat in a large flameproof casserole with a tight-fitting lid. Add the lamb and cook for 8–10 minutes, turning every few minutes until well browned. Remove the lamb.

Reheat the casserole over high heat and add the carrot, onion, garlic and bouquet garni. Reduce the heat and cook, stirring, for 8–10 minutes or until softened. Increase the heat to high and pour in the wine. Boil, stirring, for 30 seconds to deglaze, then return the lamb to the casserole. Add the stock.

Bring to the boil, then cover and reduce heat to low. Braise the meat for 1½ hours, turning twice. If the lid is not tight fitting, cover the casserole with foil and then put the lid on top.

Add the cooked beans to the lamb and return to the boil over high heat. Reduce the heat to low, cover the casserole again and cook for a further 30 minutes.

Lift the lamb out of the casserole, cover and leave to rest for 10 minutes before carving. Discard the bouquet garni. Skim the excess fat from the surface of the sauce and, if the sauce is too thin, boil over high heat for 5 minutes or until thickened slightly. Taste for seasoning. Carve the lamb and arrange on a platter. Spoon the beans around the lamb and drizzle with the sauce. Serve the rest of the sauce separately.

Baked trout with fennel and capers

This is one of those country-style dishes that is both easy and stylish. The various elements (fennel, lemon, vermouth, bay leaf) meld with the fish, perfuming it beautifully. Butter and a dash of cream thicken the cooking juices to form a light-bodied sauce.

fennel	2 bulbs, with fronds
leek	1, white part only, thickly sliced
carrot	1 large, cut into batons
olive oil	2 tablespoons
capers	2 tablespoons, rinsed and drained
French shallot	1, finely chopped
rainbow trout	4 (approx 300 g/10½ oz each)
bay leaves	1–2
butter	25 g (1 oz), cut into 4 cubes
lemon	4 slices
fish stock	185 ml (6 fl oz/¾ cup)
dry vermouth	3 tablespoons
thick (double/heavy) cream	2 tablespoons
chervil	2 tablespoons chopped

Preheat the oven to 200°C (400°F/Gas 6). Cut off the fronds from the fennel bulbs and finely chop. Thinly slice the bulbs and put in a flameproof roasting tin with the leek and carrot. Drizzle 1 tablespoon of olive oil over the vegetables, season, then toss to coat in the oil and seasoning. Roast for 20 minutes.

Mix chopped fennel fronds with the capers and shallot. Season the inside of the trout and fill with fennel and caper stuffing.

Put the bay leaves, butter and the lemon slices inside the fish. Mix together the fish stock and vermouth.

Remove the vegetables from the oven, stir well and reduce the oven to 140°C (275°F/Gas 1). Lay the trout over the vegetables and pour the stock and vermouth over the fish. Season trout and drizzle with the remaining tablespoon of olive oil. Cover top of tin with foil. Return to oven for 15–20 minutes, or until fish is cooked through. Lift the fish onto a serving platter.

Transfer roasting tin of vegetables to the stovetop and heat for a few minutes, or until the juices bubble and reduce. Add the cream and cook for 1 minute, then stir in the chervil and season to taste. Spoon the vegetables on the platter, top with the fish and pour over a little of the juice.

Fill fish cavities with the caper, fennel and shallot mixture.

Arrange trout on vegetables then add the stock and vermouth.

Pork with sage and capers

Pork fillet is a luxurious, and lean, cut of meat and here's a way to make it even more of a treat. A simple stuffing and a bacon wrapping transform it into a very elegant dish, and one that doesn't involve endless preparation either. Don't use dried sage unless you really can't get the fresh herb.

unsalted butter	25 g (1 oz)
extra virgin olive oil	3 tablespoons
onion	1, finely chopped
fresh white breadcrumbs	100 g (3½ oz/1¼ cups)
sage	2 teaspoons, chopped
flat-leaf (Italian) parsley	1 tablespoon, chopped
lemon zest	2 teaspoons grated
capers	2½ tablespoons, rinsed and drained
egg	1
pork fillets	2 large (about 500 g/1 lb 2 oz each)
bacon slices or prosciutto	8 large thin slices
plain (all-purpose) flour	2 teaspoons
dry vermouth	100 ml (3½ fl oz)
chicken or vegetable stock	315 ml (10 fl oz/1¼ cups)
sage leaves	8 whole, extra, to garnish

Preheat the oven to 170°C (325°F/Gas 3). Heat the butter and 1 tablespoon of the oil in a frying pan. Add the onion and cook for 5 minutes, or until lightly golden.

Put breadcrumbs, sage, parsley, lemon zest, the cooked onion and ½ tablespoon capers in a bowl. Add the egg, season well and mix to combine.

Using a sharp knife, split each pork fillet in half lengthways, taking care not to cut all the way through, and open out. Spread the stuffing down the length of one and cover with the other fillet.

Stretch the bacon or prosciutto with the back of a knife and wrap each piece, overlapping slices slightly, around the pork to form a neat parcel. Tie with string at regular intervals.

Place the pork in a flameproof baking dish and drizzle with 1 tablespoon of oil. Bake for 1 hour. To test if meat is cooked, insert a skewer in the thickest part; the juices should run clear. Remove meat from the dish, cover with foil and leave to rest. Place the baking dish on the stovetop, add flour and stir in well. Add the vermouth and allow to bubble for 1 minute. Add the stock and stir while cooking to remove all the lumps. Simmer for 5 minutes. Add the remaining capers to the sauce.

In a small saucepan, heat the remaining oil and when very hot, fry the sage leaves until crisp. Drain on paper towels.

Slice the pork into 2 cm (¾ in) slices. Spoon a little sauce over the pork and serve each portion with fried sage leaves.

Split the fillets lengthways and open, then spread with stuffing.

Wrap the meat in prosciutto then tie into a neat shape with string.

Entrecôte à la bordelaise

Entrecôte is a rib-eye steak although tender rump or sirloin are also appropriate to use here. Sauce bordelaise is one of the 'brown' sauces (based on beef stock) from the classic French culinary repertoire, always involving bone marrow and red wine.

sauce	
unsalted butter	50 g (1¾ oz), chilled and diced
French shallots	3, finely chopped
red wine (preferably bordeaux)	500 ml (17 fl oz/2 cups)
beef stock	250 ml (9 fl oz/1 cup)
bone marrow	80 g (2¾ oz)
flat-leaf (Italian) parsley	1 tablespoon, chopped
entrecôte or sirloin steaks	4 x 200 g (7 oz)
oil	1½ tablespoons

To make the sauce, melt 20 g (¾ oz) of the butter in a saucepan, add the shallot and cook, stirring, for 7 minutes or until very soft; do not allow shallot to brown. Pour in wine and simmer until reduced by two-thirds. Add stock and bone marrow and simmer until reduced by half, breaking up marrow as it cooks.

Whisk in the remaining pieces of butter. Season to taste with salt and pepper. Add the parsley.

Trim and season the steaks and rub with some of the oil. Heat the remaining oil in a frying pan, and cook the steaks for 2–4 minutes on each side, or until cooked to your liking. Pour the sauce over the top to serve.

French shallots are the 'gourmet' cousin to both garlic and onions. Their flavour has been described as a cross between an onion and garlic; however, this is not strictly true as they have a distinctive flavour, being milder, more refined and sweeter tasting. Shallots, like garlic, grow in a cluster that forms a bulb shape. They have papery skins which vary in colour from coppery to pink to greyish. Their size can vary from tiny to large — the large ones are easier to peel but have less flavour than the smaller types.

Tarragon chicken

SERVES 4

Tarragon cream sauce and chicken make another of those timeless combinations that simply cannot be improved upon, although the success of this dish relies heavily on the quality of the bird; use an organic or corn-fed chicken for the best results, and be sure to use French tarragon.

tarragon	1½ tablespoons, chopped
garlic	1 clove, crushed
butter	50 g (1¾ oz), softened
whole chicken	1.6 kg (3 lb 8 oz)
oil	2 teaspoons
chicken stock	150 ml (5 fl oz)
white wine	1½ tablespoons
plain (all-purpose) flour	1 tablespoon
tarragon leaves	1 tablespoon
thick (double/heavy) cream	150 ml (5 fl oz)

Preheat the oven to 200°C (400°F/Gas 6). Combine the chopped tarragon, garlic and half the butter. Season with salt and pepper and place inside the cavity of the chicken. Tie the legs together and tuck the wing tips under.

Heat the remaining butter with the oil in a large flameproof casserole dish over low heat and brown the chicken on all sides. Add the chicken stock and wine. Cover the casserole and bake in the oven for 1 hour 20 minutes, or until the chicken is tender and the juices run clear when a thigh is pierced with a skewer. Remove the chicken, draining all the juices back into the casserole dish. Cover with foil and a tea towel (dish towel) and allow to rest.

Skim a tablespoon of the surface fat from the cooking liquid and put it in a small bowl. Skim the remainder of the fat from the surface and discard. Add the flour to the reserved fat and mix until smooth. Whisk quickly into the cooking liquid and stir over medium heat until the sauce boils and thickens.

Strain the sauce into a clean saucepan and add the tarragon leaves. Simmer for 2 minutes, then stir in the cream and reheat without boiling. Season with salt and pepper. Carve chicken and spoon the sauce over the top to serve.

Tie the legs of the chicken with string and tuck the wings under.

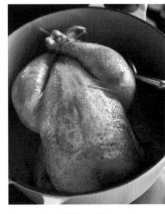

Brown the chicken all over in the butter and oil.

Pour over the stock and wine, cover then cook the chicken.

Veal paupiettes

SERVES 4

A paupiette is simply a thin slice of tender meat, or fish, wrapped around a filling then cooked. These paupiettes can be prepared (stuffed and tied) in advance then cooked at the last minute, making for an easy main course, although you will need some beef stock on hand for the sauce.

stuffing

butter	30 g (1 oz)
French shallots	2, finely chopped
garlic	1 clove, crushed
minced (ground) pork	200 g (7 oz)
minced (ground) veal	200 g (7 oz)
egg	1
dry white wine	2 tablespoons
fresh white breadcrumbs	3 tablespoons
flat-leaf (Italian) parsley	2 tablespoons, finely chopped
veal escalopes	4 x 150 g (5½ oz), pounded flat

sauce

clarified butter	30 g (1 oz)
onion	1, diced
carrot	1, diced
celery	1 stalk, diced
white wine	100 ml (3½ fl oz)
tomato paste (concentrated purée)	2 teaspoons
bay leaf	1
beef stock	350 ml (12 fl oz)

To make stuffing, melt butter in a saucepan and cook shallots over low heat until softened but not browned. Add garlic and cook for a further 2 minutes, then set aside to cool. Mix with other stuffing ingredients and season with salt and pepper.

Lay the veal escalopes flat and spread evenly with the stuffing, leaving a narrow border around the edge. Roll up the paupiettes, then tie with kitchen string at regular intervals.

To make sauce, melt half the clarified butter in a frying pan. Add the onion, carrot and celery and cook over low heat until softened. Increase heat to brown vegetables. Remove from pan.

Heat the remaining clarified butter in the frying pan and brown the paupiettes, turning once. Remove from the pan, pour in the white wine and boil, stirring, for 30 seconds. Add the tomato paste and bay leaf. Pour in the stock and bring to a simmer before adding the vegetables and paupiettes.

Cover the pan and cook for 12–15 minutes, or until a skewer inserted into the centre of a paupiette comes out too hot to touch. Remove the paupiettes from the pan and keep warm.

Strain the sauce. Return the sauce to the pan and boil until reduced by half and syrupy. Slice each paupiette into five pieces and serve with a little sauce poured over the top.

After pounding flat, spread the escalopes evenly with filling.

Roll the escalopes up then tie securely with kitchen string.

Quails with grapes and tarragon

Quails are a little gamey but not overly so and as they are lean, they are best cooked medium or medium–rare — otherwise they will be dry and tough. Reducing the cooking liquid by rapid boiling is a classic french technique and produces a deeply-flavoured, light-bodied sauce.

tarragon	8 sprigs
quails	8 x 150 g (5½ oz)
clarified butter	2 tablespoons
white wine	150 ml (5½ fl oz)
chicken stock	400 ml (14 fl oz)
green grapes	150 g (5½ oz) seedless

Put a sprig of tarragon into the cavity of each quail and season quails well. Heat the clarified butter in a sauté pan or deep frying pan and brown the quails on all sides. Add the wine and boil for 30 seconds, then add the stock and grapes.

Cover the pan and simmer for 8 minutes or until the quails are just cooked through. Lift out the quails and grapes and keep warm. Boil the sauce until it has reduced by two-thirds and become syrupy. Strain the sauce and pour over the quails and grapes to serve.

Tarragon is associated with French cookery more than it is any other cuisine. In France it is an essential flavouring in the famous Sauce Bearnaise, is a component of the fines herbes mix and lends its unmistakable fragrance to myriad sauces, stews and salad dressings as well as appearing in mustards and pickles. With its strong, peppery, licorice flavour and aroma, tarragon should be used sparingly as it can quickly overpower a dish. It has special affinity for chicken and fish. An excellent way to preserve fresh tarragon is to steep bruised sprigs of the herb in white wine vinegar — this becomes an excellent base for vinaigrettes and a wonderful addition to egg, chicken or fish poaching liquid.

Pork noisettes with prunes

The Touraine region of France is renowned for its honest, home-style cooking that is typified by simple combinations. Pork marries with prunes as beautifully as it does with apples, which are some of the few fruit-with-meat combinations the French repertoire seems to sanction.

pork fillets	2 x 400 g (14 oz)
prunes	16, pitted
vegetable oil	1 tablespoon
butter	45 g (1½ oz)
onion	1, finely chopped
white wine	155 ml (5 fl oz)
chicken or beef stock	280 ml (9½ fl oz)
bay leaf	1
thyme	2 sprigs
thick (double/heavy) cream	250 ml (9 fl oz/1 cup)

Trim the pork, removing any membrane. Cut each fillet into four diagonal slices. Put the prunes in a small saucepan, cover with cold water and bring to the boil. Reduce the heat and simmer the prunes for 5 minutes. Drain well.

Heat the oil in a large heavy-based saucepan and add half the butter. When the butter starts foaming, add the pork, in batches if necessary, and sauté on both sides until cooked. Transfer the pork to a warm plate, cover and keep warm.

Pour off the excess fat from the pan. Melt remaining butter, add the onion and cook over low heat until softened but not browned. Add the wine, bring to the boil and simmer for 2 minutes. Add the stock, bay leaf and thyme and bring to the boil. Reduce the heat and simmer for 10 minutes or until reduced by half.

Strain the stock into a bowl and rinse the frying pan. Return stock to the pan, add the cream and prunes and simmer for 8 minutes, or until the sauce thickens slightly. Return the pork to the pan and simmer until heated through.

Cook the pork in batches until cooked but still slightly pink.

Simmer the prune sauce gently to reduce and thicken it slightly.

vegetables and salads

France has a strong agricultural heritage; an abundance of vegetables is grown across a variety of climatic conditions and so, not surprisingly, French cuisine offers up a multitude of ways to prepare these. It is important to understand that the French do not consider vegetables to be mere fillers on a main-course plate, many of their vegetable dishes are intended to be savoured as a separate course. Often, just one vegetable dish, or salad, is served on its own and near the end of a meal. The rationale is a sound one — eating the vegetable or salad component alone allows textures to be fully appreciated and, served in this way, the vegetable dish provides contrast and balance to the overall meal. Often, bread will accompany a main meal so potatoes are not always considered necessary, as they tend to be in Anglo-Saxon dining. Essentially, there are two main methods used in French cuisine for cooking green vegetables — *à l'anglaise*, which involves blanching or cooking in a large quantity of water, and *à la français*, where vegetables are slowly cooked in a covered saucepan and in the minimum of liquid. Many vegetables are slow-cooked, including unexpected candidates such as lettuce, green peas and beans. When prepared in this way, vegetables will not be bright green and crunchy, but any loss of vibrant colour is more than compensated by the beautifully deep, sweet flavours acquired through slow, patient simmering.

Many of the most memorable vegetable preparations are the simplest and therefore, it almost goes without saying, rely for success on the best seasonal produce you can find. It's always worth shelling fresh peas, washing fresh English spinach and hunting down snappy, farm-fresh asparagus and green beans, but even more so when preparing them in the French style. The rewards of waiting until summer comes until preparing anything involving raw tomatoes is the intense flavour and rich juiciness that year-round supply has made us all but forget.

French salads are restrained, simple affairs with often just a few, carefully-chosen, complementary ingredients used. The aim is to be able to savour all the elements, without any one ingredient taking over. French salads are studies in textural contrast too, with ingredients such as semi-soft cheeses, olives or oranges providing soft textures and sharp flavours; nuts and lardons of bacon add richness (as do oil-based dressings) and strips of raw vegetables or cubes of toasted bread are added for crunch. Although simple, such salads demand care in preparation. Tender green leaves should be gently washed and dried (a salad spinner is good for this), then tossed with dressing just before serving.

Braised witlof

Witlof, chicory or Belgian endive as it is also known, is regarded as a salad vegetable. However, when braised with stock, butter and a dash of cream, it takes on a different character. This dish is worthy of a dinner party, where it could be served as the vegetable dish, or as a hot entrée.

witlof (chicory/Belgian endive)	8 heads
butter	20 g (¾ oz)
soft brown sugar	1 teaspoon
tarragon vinegar	2 teaspoons
chicken stock	1oo ml (3½ fl oz)
thick (double/heavy) cream	2 tablespoons

Trim the ends from the witlof. Melt the butter in a deep frying pan and fry the witlof briefly on all sides. Add sugar, vinegar and chicken stock and bring to the boil. Reduce the heat to a simmer and cover the pan.

Simmer gently for 30 minutes, or until tender, turning halfway through. Take the lid off the pan and simmer until nearly all the liquid has evaporated. Stir in the cream and serve.

This is also commonly called chicory or Belgian endive, although the Belgians themselves call it witlof. Whatever one calls it, witlof is delicious, with a crisp texture and a refreshingly bitter edge to its flavour. Most commonly used as a salad green, witlof is well-suited to braising, becoming soft and mellow over the long, slow cooking. Choose heads of witlof that are tight and compact with pale yellow tips and with minimal greening on the exterior — when exposed to light, witlof starts to turn green which is also an indication of bitterness. Witlof should be stored for 1–2 days only and should be wrapped to guard against bruising and refrigerated in a plastic bag.

Lentils in red wine

Lentils are a humble, nourishing food and when cooked in this way, are elevated to something special. In this recipe, French *lentilles vertes du puy* (the prized lentils from the village of Le Puy) are specified but you could substitute regular brown lentils, which will be easier to find.

olive oil	2 tablespoons
celery	1 stick, finely diced
carrot	1 large, finely diced
onion	1 large, finely diced
garlic cloves	2, crushed
tomato paste (concentrated purée)	2 tablespoons
puy lentils	280 g (10 oz/1½ cups)
red wine	250 ml (9 fl oz/1 cup)
beef stock	250 ml (9 fl oz/1 cup)
bay leaf	1, crushed
thyme	5 sprigs
flat-leaf (Italian) parsley	3 tablespoons, chopped

Heat the olive oil in a large heavy-based saucepan. Add the celery, carrot and onion and cook over medium–low heat for 10 minutes. Add the garlic and cook for a further 2 minutes.

Add the tomato paste and cook over low heat for 5 minutes. Stir in the lentils, then add wine and cook over medium heat for 3–5 minutes, until slightly reduced. Add stock and 375 ml (12 fl oz/1½ cups) water, bring to the boil, then reduce heat and add the herbs. Season and simmer for 45–50 minutes, until the liquid is absorbed and the lentils are cooked. Stir in the parsley and then serve.

Cut the vegetables into small, even-sized pieces.

Add the lentils to the softened vegetables and tomato paste.

Peas with onions and lettuce

SERVES 6

Cooking vegetables this way — in a little liquid and for a comparatively long time — intensifies their flavour and renders them pleasingly soft. Even lettuce is cooked like this, resulting in tender leaves that complement the other ingredients perfectly.

butter	50 g (1¾ oz)
baby onions or French shallots	16
peas	500 g (1 lb 2 oz) fresh, shelled
iceberg lettuce heart	250 g (9 oz), finely shredded
flat-leaf (Italian) parsley	2 sprigs
caster (superfine) sugar	1 teaspoon
chicken stock	125 ml (4 fl oz/½ cup)
plain (all-purpose) flour	1 tablespoon

Melt 30 g (1 oz) of the butter in a large saucepan. Add the onions and cook, stirring, for 1 minute. Add the peas, lettuce, parsley sprigs and sugar. Pour in the stock and stir well. Cover the pan and cook over medium–low heat for 15 minutes, stirring occasionally, until the onions are cooked through. Remove the parsley.

Mix the remaining butter with the flour. Add small amounts to the vegetables, stirring until the juices thicken a little. Season well with salt and black pepper.

Thanks to the availability of frozen peas, we tend to forget the joys of seasonal peas, podded by hand and cooked fresh. It's true though, that peas do freeze better than most vegetables and these are indeed a viable alternative when fresh are simply unavailable; after all the season for fresh, tender, spring peas is fleeting. Choose fresh peas with pods that are bright green and snapping crisp — avoid those which show signs of yellowing or have large peas within the pod as these will be starchy. The sugars inside the peas start converting to starch very soon after harvesting so buy them young and store them as briefly as possible (in the refrigerator) before cooking them.

Roasted fennel and orange salad

SERVES 4

Baby fennel bulbs taste mild and sweet and oven-roasting accentuates their subtle, aniseed flavours. Orange, olives and mint add summery, vibrant touches to this wonderful salad which makes a refreshing course after a lamb, duck or beef dish.

fennel	8 small bulbs
olive oil	100 ml (3½ fl oz)
oranges	2
lemon juice	1 tablespoon
red onion	1, halved and thinly sliced
kalamata olives	100 g (3½ oz)
mint	2 tablespoons, roughly chopped
flat-leaf (Italian) parsley	1 tablespoon, roughly chopped

Preheat the oven to 200°C (400°F/Gas 6). Trim the fronds from the fennel and reserve. Remove the stalks and cut a slice off the base of each fennel bulb about 5 mm (¼ in) thick. Slice each bulb into 6 wedges, place in a baking dish and then drizzle with 3 tablespoons olive oil. Season well. Bake for 40–45 minutes, or until the fennel is tender and slightly caramelized. Turn once or twice during cooking. Allow to cool.

Cut a thin slice off the top and bottom of each orange. Using a small sharp knife, slice the skin and pith off the oranges, removing as much pith as possible. Slice down the side of a segment between the flesh and the membrane. Repeat with the other side and lift the segment out. Do this over a bowl to catch the juices. Repeat with all the segments on both oranges. Squeeze any juice remaining in the membranes into the bowl.

Whisk the remaining oil into the orange juice and the lemon juice and season well. Combine the orange segments, onion and olives in a bowl, pour over half the dressing and add half the mint. Mix well. Transfer to a serving dish. Top with the roasted fennel, drizzle with the remaining dressing, and scatter the parsley and remaining mint over the top. Chop the reserved fronds and sprinkle over the salad.

Arrange the fennel wedges in a single layer in a roasting dish.

Use a knife to remove the orange segments from the membrane.

three ways with potatoes

Generations of French cooks have made an art of potato cookery, inventing simple, delicious ways to serve this ubiquitous vegetable. Pommes anna is essentially a potato 'cake' but one the French take so seriously they even have a special pan for making it. Use floury rather than waxy potatoes for gratin dauphinois as they will better absorb the cooking liquid than waxy ones and give a fluffier result. Boulangère potatoes (translating as 'in the style of the bakers' wife') are meltingly tender under their golden, crisp top; use a good home-made stock for these.

BOULANGÈRE POTATOES

Preheat the oven to 180°C (350°F/Gas 4). Thinly slice 1 kg (2 lb 4 oz) all-purpose potatoes and 1 large onion with a mandolin or sharp knife. Make alternate layers of potato and onion in a 20 x 10 cm (8 x 4 in) deep dish, sprinkling 2 tablespoons finely chopped flat-leaf (Italian) parsley, salt and black pepper between each layer. Finish with a layer of potato. Pour 500 ml (17 fl oz/2 cups) hot chicken stock over the top and dot with 25 g (1 oz) butter, cubed. Bake, covered with foil, on the middle shelf of the oven for 30 minutes, then remove the foil and press down on the potatoes to keep them submerged in the stock. Bake for a further 30 minutes, or until the potatoes are tender and the top golden brown. Serve piping hot. Serves 6.

GRATIN DAUPHINOIS

Preheat the oven to 170°C (325°F/Gas 3). Thinly slice 1 kg (2 lb 4 oz) floury potatoes with a mandolin or sharp knife. Butter a 23 x 16 cm (9 x 6¼ in) ovenproof dish and layer the potatoes, sprinkling 2 crushed garlic cloves, 75 g (2½ oz) gruyère cheese, grated, a pinch of nutmeg and seasoning between the layers, leaving a little of the cheese for the top. Pour 300 ml (10½ fl oz) thick (double/heavy) cream and 100 ml (3½ fl oz) milk over the top and sprinkle with the cheese. Bake for 50–60 minutes, or until the potatoes are completely cooked and the liquid absorbed. If the top browns too much, cover loosely with foil. Leave to rest for 10 minutes before serving. Serves 6.

POMMES ANNA

Preheat the oven to 210°C (415°F/Gas 6–7). Grease a deep 20 cm (8 in) round cake tin or ovenproof dish with melted butter. Peel 850 g (1 lb 14 oz) waxy potatoes and cut into very thin slices with a mandolin or sharp knife. Lay the potato slices on paper towels and pat dry. Starting from the centre of the dish, overlap one-fifth of the potato slices over the base. Drizzle 25 g (1 oz) of clarified butter over the top. Season well. Repeat the layers four more times, drizzling the remaining butter over the top. Cut a circle of greaseproof paper to fit over the top of the potato. Bake for about 1 hour, or until cooked and golden and a knife blade slides easily into the centre. Remove from oven and leave for 5 minutes, then pour off any excess butter. Run a knife around the edge to loosen, then turn out onto a serving plate. Serves 4.

boulangère potatoes

Salade au chèvre

SERVES 4

Chèvre is goat's cheese, which has pleasant, tangy flavours and a soft, smooth texture. Chèvre teams beautifully with the rich crunch of toasted walnuts and the freshness of salad greens. This salad works best when plated individually rather than served from a large bowl.

walnuts	50 g (1¾ oz), broken into pieces
flaked sea salt	1 teaspoon
baguette	8 slices
garlic	1 clove, cut in half
chèvre	125 g (4½ oz), cut into 8 slices
mesclun (mixed salad leaves and herbs)	50 g (1¾ oz)
red onion	1 small, thinly sliced

dressing

olive oil	2 tablespoons
walnut oil	1 tablespoon
tarragon vinegar	1½ tablespoons
garlic	1 clove, crushed

Preheat the grill (broiler) to hot. Put the walnuts in a bowl and cover with boiling water. Leave for 1 minute, then drain and shake dry. Toast under the grill for 3–4 minutes, or until golden. Sprinkle sea salt over top, toss lightly and allow to cool.

Put the baguette slices under the grill and toast one side until lightly golden. Remove from the heat and rub the toasted side with the cut garlic. Leave for a few minutes to cool and crisp, then turn over and place a slice of chèvre on each. Grill for 2–3 minutes, or until the cheese browns.

To make the dressing, combine the olive oil, walnut oil, vinegar and garlic and season well.

Toss the mesclun, onion and toasted walnuts together on a large platter. Arrange the chèvre croutons on top and drizzle with the dressing. Serve while the croutons are still warm.

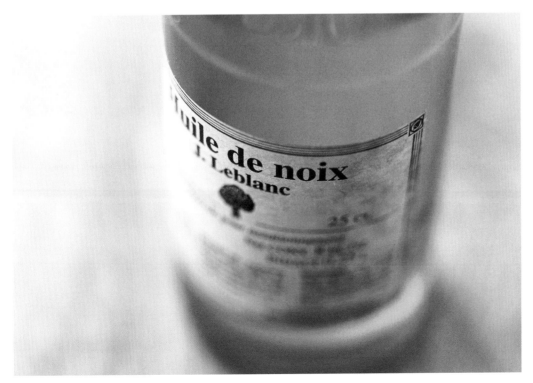

Walnut oil, or huile de noix in French, is extracted from fresh, roasted walnuts (make sure the label states roasted walnuts have been used as some producers cheat and omit this crucial step). Light brown in colour, good walnut oil is expensive and should be purchased in small quantities as it is highly perishable. However, the rich, nutty flavour is without equal, especially when used in salad dressings as it is in this recipe. In fact, this oil is not a cooking oil at all as high heat destroys its flavour; it is at its best in dressings, sauces and when used in baking. Store walnut oil in a cool, dark place or in the refrigerator, and use within 3 months of opening.

Ratatouille

Be sure to make ratatouille in the summer months, when basil, zucchini (courgettes) and tomatoes are at their best. There are many ways to prepare this dish. Here, the vegetables are sautéed separately before being simmered together — this may seem laborious but it is worth it.

tomatoes	4
olive oil	2 tablespoons
onion	1 large, diced
red capsicum (pepper)	1, diced
yellow capsicum (pepper)	1, diced
eggplant (aubergine)	1, diced
zucchini (courgettes)	2, diced
tomato paste (concentrated purée)	1 teaspoon
sugar	½ teaspoon
bay leaf	1
thyme sprigs	3 sprigs
basil sprigs	2 sprigs
garlic clove	1, crushed
flat-leaf (Italian) parsley	1 tablespoon chopped

Score a cross in the base of each tomato, plunge into boiling water for 20 seconds and then peel the skin away from the cross. Roughly chop.

Heat the oil in a frying pan. Add the onion and cook over low heat for 5 minutes. Add the capsicum and cook, stirring, for 4 minutes. Remove from the pan and set aside.

Fry eggplant until lightly browned all over and then remove from the pan. Fry the zucchini until browned and then return the onion, capsicum and eggplant to the pan. Add the tomato paste, stir well and cook for 2 minutes. Add tomato, sugar, bay leaf, thyme and basil. Stir well, cover and cook for 15 minutes. Remove the bay leaf, thyme and basil.

Mix together the garlic and parsley and add to the ratatouille at the last minute. Stir and serve.

Before dicing capsicums, remove ribs, membranes and seeds.

Sauté the vegetables separately as cooking times vary.

Tian de legumes

SERVES 6–8

A tian is a shallow, earthenware cooking vessel that, like a casserole, has given its name to the dish that is cooked in it; traditionally people took their tian to the local baker's to slowly cook in their oven. Tians are also delicious when topped and baked with a scattering of cheese and crumbs.

sweet potato	500 g (1 lb 2 oz)
all-purpose potatoes	1.25 kg (2 lb 12 oz)
leeks	4 large
garlic	3 cloves
nutmeg	¾ teaspoon
bay leaves	3
cream (whipping)	300 ml (10½ fl oz)

Preheat the oven to 170°C (325°F/Gas 3) and grease a 26 x 28 x 7 cm (10 x 11 x 3 in) tian or shallow, ovenproof ceramic dish. Peel and thinly slice the sweet potato and the potatoes using a mandoline or large, sharp knife. Slice leeks into thin rings. Thinly slice the garlic.

Layer half the potatoes over the base of the prepared dish. Scatter over a few slices of garlic and add a bay leaf. Sprinkle lightly with salt and pepper, and ¼ teaspoon of the nutmeg. Scatter the leeks, some garlic slices and a bay leaf over the top, and sprinkle with salt and pepper and ¼ teaspoon of nutmeg. Layer the sweet potato, some garlic slices and a bay leaf and season as above with salt, pepper and nutmeg. Layer with the remaining potatoes, season and pour the cream over.

Cover with foil and bake for 2½–3 hours, or until vegetables are very tender. After 2 hours, remove the foil to allow the top to become crisp and golden. Remove from the oven and rest for 5 minutes before serving.

A mandoline makes quick work of slicing vegetables.

Neatly layer the vegetables in the dish.

the perfect
hollandaise sauce

Hollandaise sauce is one of the defining dishes of French gastronomy and many a chef is judged by the quality of his, or her, hollandaise. When expertly-made, this sauce is airy, subtly-flavoured and rich, and can be spooned over steamed asparagus, or served with poached eggs, steamed or poached white meats or fish. The key to this sauce lies in knowing when to stop whisking the egg yolks and water-based liquid; this first emulsion is known as a sabayon. As the egg is whisked, it will increase in volume. When it stiffens slightly, immediately start adding the butter.

Cut 180 g (6 oz) unsalted butter into cubes then melt and bring to a simmer in a saucepan. Remove from the heat, skim any scum from surface then cool for a few minutes. Carefully decant butter into a jug, taking care to leave all the white milk solids behind; discard solids.

Half-fill a saucepan with water and bring to a simmer. Combine 3 egg yolks, 1 tablespoon of lemon juice, 2 teaspoons white wine vinegar and 1 tablespoon of water in a heatproof bowl and whisk. Place bowl over simmering water, making sure it does not touch water, then whisk the mixture constantly for 1–2 minutes or until thick, foamy, and increased in volume. Remove from the heat and then whisk for 20 seconds or so to cool slightly then gradually whisk in butter. Season and serve warm. Serves 4.

Salade niçoise

SERVES 4

Debate rages over what constitutes an 'authentic' salade niçoise — even in Provence, the home of the dish, variations abound and opinions differ. Whoever is 'right', one thing is for certain — salade niçoise should sing with the sunny, salty flavours of the Southern French coast.

waxy potatoes	4
olive oil	1 tablespoon
green beans	200 g (7 oz) small, halved
tuna	300 g (10½ oz) tinned, in oil, drained
lettuce leaves	200 g (7 oz)
cherry tomatoes	150 g (5½ oz), halved
black olives	20, pitted
capers	2 tablespoons
hard-boiled eggs	3, cut into wedges
anchovy fillets	8

vinaigrette

garlic	1 clove, crushed
dijon mustard	1 teaspoon
white wine vinegar	2 tablespoons
lemon juice	1 teaspoon
olive oil	125 ml (4 fl oz/½ cup)

Cook the potatoes in boiling salted water for 15 minutes, or until just tender. Drain, cut into small cubes and place in a bowl. Drizzle with the olive oil and toss well. Cook the green beans in boiling salted water for 3 minutes, then drain. Refresh under cold water, then drain well.

To make the vinaigrette, whisk together the garlic, mustard, vinegar and lemon juice. Add the oil in a thin steady stream, whisking until smooth.

Put the tuna in a bowl and separate into large chunks with a fork. Cover the base of a serving dish with the lettuce leaves. Scatter the potatoes, beans, tuna, tomatoes, olives and capers over the leaves, pour the vinaigrette over the top and decorate with the egg and anchovies.

Capers are the immature flower buds of a plant that favours dry, coastal conditions such as those that exist along the Mediterranean coast of the South of France. Bland when raw, capers require curing or pickling in order for their distinctive peppery, mustardy flavour to fully develop. Hence they are purchased either pickled in vinegar or preserved in salt; those in salt tend to have better flavour and require soaking in warm water before use.

Capers add their zing to many dishes and are a distinctive feature of southern French cooking. There are various grades of caper — the most prized are the smallest as these have the finest, and most intense, flavour.

Fennel, tomato and garlic gratin

SERVES 4

All the wonderful flavours of the various vegetables used here meld together when baked under a crisp, tasty topping; a gratin is a favourite provencal treatment for vegetables. Make this in summer when tomatoes are at their juicy best.

fennel bulbs	1 kg (2 lb 4 oz)
olive oil	4 tablespoons
red onion	1 large, halved and thinly sliced
garlic	2 cloves, crushed
tomatoes	500 g (1 lb 2 oz)

gratin topping

white bread	60 g (2¼ oz), broken into coarse crumbs
parmesan cheese	65 g (2¼ oz), grated
lemon zest	2 teaspoons, grated
garlic clove	1, crushed

Preheat the oven to 200°C (400°F/Gas 6). Grease a gratin dish with melted butter or oil. Cut the fennel in half lengthways, then slice thinly.

Heat oil in a large frying pan. Cook onion for 3–4 minutes until softened but not browned. Add the garlic and cook for 2 minutes. Add fennel and cook, stirring frequently, for about 7 minutes, or until softened and lightly golden brown.

Score a cross in the base of each tomato, plunge into boiling water for 20 seconds and then peel skin away from the cross. Chop roughly and add to the fennel. Cook, stirring frequently, for 5 minutes, or until the tomato is softened. Season well and pour into the gratin dish.

To make the gratin topping, mix together all the ingredients, sprinkle over the vegetables and bake for 15 minutes, or until golden brown and crisp. Serve immediately.

Once fennel and other vegetables are soft, add the tomato.

Sprinkle the topping in a thick layer over the vegetables.

Salade aux noix

This effortless preparation can easily go one of two ways — it can be dull and ordinary... or sensational. With such an uncomplicated dish, the difference lies in the selection of ingredients. Make sure you buy walnuts loose, so you can taste them first and check they are sweet.

baguette	4 thin slices
garlic	1 clove, cut in half
olive oil	4 tablespoons
butter lettuce	1 large
walnut oil	25 ml (1 fl oz)
red wine vinegar	25 ml (1 fl oz)
dijon mustard	1 teaspoon
walnuts	70 g (2½ oz), broken into pieces
bacon slices	150 g (5½ oz), cut into small pieces

Preheat the grill (broiler) and rub the baguette with the cut garlic. Drizzle a little of the olive oil on each side of the bread and then grill until golden brown. Leave to cool.

Tear lettuce leaves into pieces and arrange on a large platter. Mix together the remaining olive oil, walnut oil, vinegar and mustard and season to make a dressing.

Put the walnuts in a bowl and cover with boiling water. Leave for 1 minute, drain and shake dry.

Cook the bacon in a frying pan until crisp, then remove from pan with a slotted spoon and sprinkle over the lettuce. Add the walnuts to the pan and cook for a few minutes until browned, then add to the salad. Pour dressing into pan and heat through.

Pour the dressing over the salad and toss well. Add the garlic croutons to serve.

Take care not to burn the walnuts — shake the pan often.

Make sure lettuce leaves are dry so the dressing will cling to them.

Purée of spinach

SERVES 4

Just a little butter and crème frâiche do wonders for spinach. If you can, though, grate your own nutmeg as the result will be more fragrant than if using pre-ground. Serve this vegetable side dish with grilled or poached fish, roasted lamb or grilled cutlets or steak.

English spinach leaves	1 kg (2 lb 4 oz)
butter	50 g (1¾ oz), cubed
crème fraîche	4 tablespoons
nutmeg	½ teaspoon

Wash the spinach and put in a large saucepan with just the water clinging to the leaves. Cover and steam for 2 minutes, or until just wilted. Drain, cool and squeeze dry with your hands. Finely chop.

Put the spinach in a small saucepan and gently heat through. Increase heat and, stirring constantly, gradually add the butter. Add the crème fraîche and nutmeg and stir into the spinach to combine. Season well and serve immediately.

Crème fraîche originated in Brittany and Normandy and is now used all over France. It is essentially a sour cream product, made using unpasteurised cream, which naturally contains the bacteria required to thicken it. With its thick texture and tangy flavour, it is highly prized in French cooking as, unlike sour cream, it can be boiled without curdling and can be whipped to top desserts. Sour cream can be substituted but the flavour is not the same — you can make your own crème fraîche by combining 250 ml (9 fl oz/1 cup) cream (whipping) with 2 tablespoons buttermilk. Stand the mixture, covered, at room temperature until thickened (12–24 hours) then refrigerate. Use within 10 days.

desserts

The French adore the sweet course and love to indulge, without guilt, in the creamy, rich confections for which their dessert repertoire is so famed. They weave magic with the simplest of ingredients (flour, eggs, sugar) but take great care to use only quality ingredients for optimum results. Thus butter (never margarine), fresh eggs, chocolate with a high cocoa butter content, vanilla beans or extract (not essence), the better brands of liqueur and only the most flavoursome fruits should be employed to replicate seductive treats worthy of Lyons, Strasbourg or Paris. We take pastry for granted — indeed, we consider it everyday fare — yet over centuries the French refined the concept of a 'short' dough, giving us the meltingly buttery, sweet and crisp substance we have today. Similarly, crème caramel, chocolate mousse and crêpes suzettes are well-known favourites yet are nothing short of revelatory when carefully prepared and cooked. Some classic French desserts, such as crème brûlée, for example, have become culinary clichés and perhaps no longer considered 'fashionable' — for the French, though, such a concept is nonsensical. For them, a great dish is timeless and never becomes passé.

The French are masters of culinary understatement — seemingly artless, homey dishes, such as cherry clafoutis and poached pears possess both a sophistication and an ability to satisfy, that make them truly special.

The concept, though, of a progressive menu where sweet foods are served at the meal's end, is a relatively modern one — it wasn't really until halfway through the nineteenth century, when sugar became affordable and widely available, that a separate dessert course became the norm in Europe. Before this, it was common practice to pile tables high, buffet-style, with haunches of meat sitting cheek-by-jowl with honey (or sugar) sweetened dishes and diners would eat a little of everything — together and at the same time! Thanks to the innovation of service à la Russe, or the system of serving subsequent courses in the order one was most likely to want to eat them, we now have that most anticipated of courses —the dessert — with all the skills and inventiveness that go into creating it. It is important, when deciding which dessert to serve, to consider what has come before it and balance flavours, richness and textures with previous courses. For example, avoid serving a cream-based dessert such as crème brûlée if a dairy-rich main course has been on the menu. Similarly, if the main course has been a hearty dish, make the dessert a fruit-based one, or at least something very light. If you really want to indulge in a memorably rich dessert, then serve a simple grill (fish or chicken, perhaps) or even a main-course salad, before doing so.

Coffee crémets with chocolate sauce

SERVES 4

Crémets are a simple combination of cream cheese, sugar, cream and, sometimes, egg white. Here, this time-honoured recipe is given an extra dimension by the inclusion of the wonderful mocha flavours of coffee and chocolate.

cream cheese	250 g (9 oz)
thick (double/heavy) cream	250 ml (9 fl oz/1 cup)
strong brewed coffee	4 tablespoons, cooled
caster (superfine) sugar	80 g (2¾ oz/⅓ cup)

chocolate sauce

dark chocolate	100 g (3½ oz)
unsalted butter	50 g (1¾ oz)

Line four 100 ml (3½ oz) perforated ceramic ramekins or heart-shaped moulds with muslin, leaving enough muslin hanging over the side to wrap over the crémet. Place ramekins on a tray.

Beat the cream cheese until smooth, then whisk in the cream. Add the coffee and sugar and mix. Pour into the ramekins and fold the muslin over the top. Refrigerate for at least 1½ hours. Unwrap the muslin and turn the crémets out onto individual plates, carefully peeling the muslin off.

To make the chocolate sauce, gently melt the chocolate in a saucepan with the butter and 4 tablespoons of water. Stir until combined well and until the mixture is glossy. Allow to cool slightly. Pour a little chocolate sauce over each crémet and serve immediately.

Cut pieces of muslin and use them to line the moulds.

Cool the coffee mixture before adding it to the cheese.

Pour mixture into the moulds then bring the muslin over the tops.

Pears in red wine

SERVES 6

Simple, but impossible to improve upon, this dessert is yet another timeless favourite from the French dessert repertoire. Select firm but ripe pears of similar size so they all cook to tenderness at the same time and, if desired, use an apple corer to remove the core before poaching.

arrowroot	1 tablespoon
red wine	750 ml (26 gl oz/3 cups)
sugar	110 g (3¾ oz)
cinnamon	1 stick
cloves	6
orange zest	1 tablespoons, grated
lemon zest	1 tablespoons, grated
pears	6 (ripe but still firm)

Mix the arrowroot with 2 tablespoons of the wine and set aside. Heat the remaining wine in a saucepan with the sugar, cinnamon stick, cloves and orange and lemon zest. Simmer gently for a few minutes, stirring occasionally, until the sugar has dissolved.

Peel pears, but don't remove the stalks. Put the whole pears in the saucepan of wine, cover and poach gently for 25 minutes, or until they are very tender, turning occasionally. Lift out with a slotted spoon and place on serving plates.

Strain the wine mixture, discarding solids, then pour back into the saucepan. Stir the arrowroot mixture and add to the hot wine. Simmer gently, stirring occasionally, until thickened. Pour over the pears and stand until cooled. Serve with cream or crème fraîche.

Pears reached their zenith of popularity in seventeenth century France where they were considered the most regal of fruits. King Louis XIV had much to do with this; he adored pears and many a noble found favour at his court by developing some new variety for his enjoyment. Indeed, the French are responsible for some of the varieties we know and most love today. The perfect pear for this recipe is the Beurre Bosc. Peel away the greenish-brown skin and discover the firm, creamy, and aromatic flesh which keeps its shape extremely well when cooked. Or use the diminutive corella pear (pictured), which also has excellent flavour.

Chocolate-hazelnut cake

SERVES 10–12

This is one of those unfussy cakes that exhibit plenty of flavour and loads of finesse — the sort that the French do so well. Rich, yet light in texture, this cake has no flour; the ground nuts provide body and subtle flavour. If preferred, you may use ground almonds instead of hazelnuts.

unsalted butter	150 g (5½ oz), chopped
dark chocolate	175 g (6 oz), chopped
eggs	8, separated
caster (superfine) sugar	200 g (7 oz)
vanilla extract	1 teaspoon
unsweetened cocoa powder	40 g (1½ oz/⅓ cup), sifted
ground hazelnut	250 g (9 oz/2 cups)

ganache
cream (whipping)	250 ml (9 fl oz/1 cup)
dark chocolate	200 g (7 oz), chopped

Preheat the oven to 180°C (350°F/Gas 4). Lightly grease and flour a 24 cm (9½ in) spring-form pan.

Combine the butter and chocolate in a bowl and set over a saucepan of simmering water, making sure base of bowl doesn't touch the water. Stir until melted. Remove from heat and stir until smooth and well combined. Allow to cool slightly.

Combine egg yolks, sugar and vanilla in a bowl. Using electric beaters, whisk until mixture is thick and pale. Add chocolate mixture and stir until smooth. Add cocoa and ground hazelnut and stir until well combined.

Whisk the egg whites in a large bowl until firm peaks form. Stir a quarter of the egg whites into the chocolate mixture, then gently fold the remaining egg whites into the mixture until well combined.

Pour the mixture into the prepared pan and bake for 1 hour, or until firm to touch. Allow to cool in the pan for 15 minutes, then turn out onto a wire rack to cool completely.

To make the ganache, put cream in a saucepan and bring to the boil. Put the chocolate in a bowl and add the cream. Stir until the chocolate is melted and the mixture is smooth. Refrigerate ganache until cooled and beginning to thicken. Whisk until ganache thickens slightly, then spread over the cooled cake.

This cake can be stored in an airtight container in the refrigerator for up to three days.

Stir the melted chocolate into the whisked egg yolk mixture.

Add the combined cocoa and ground hazelnut and stir well.

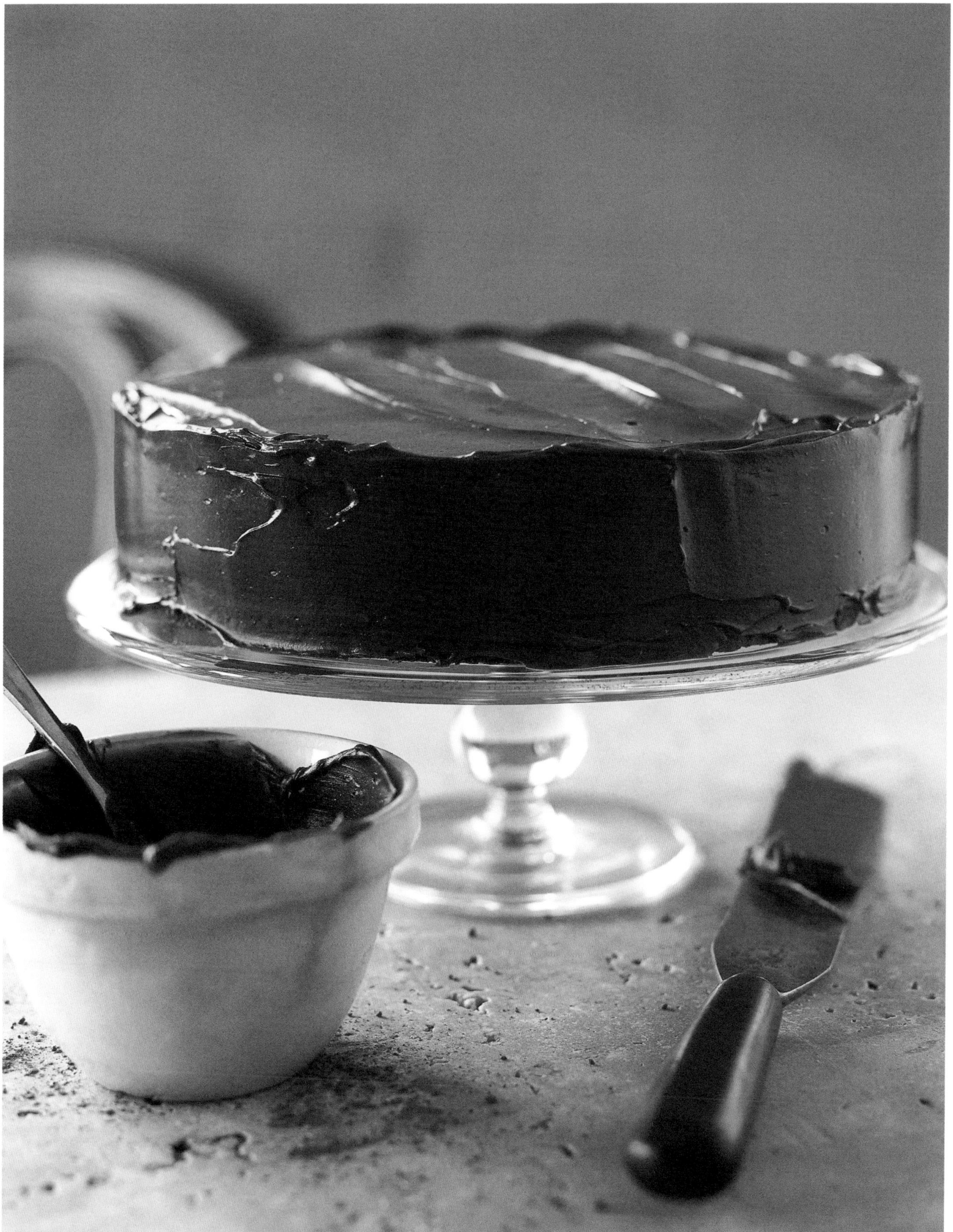

Chocolate mousse

Here's another dessert that never goes out of date or style. To achieve a guaranteed sublime result, use a bitter-sweet chocolate with 70% cocoa solids and don't over-whip the cream or it may curdle as you fold it through, making your mousse grainy and dry.

good quality dark chocolate	300 g (10½ oz), chopped
unsalted butter	30 g (1 oz), chopped
eggs	2, lightly beaten
Cognac	3 tablespoons
egg whites	4
caster (superfine) sugar	100 g (3½ oz)
cream (whipping)	500 ml (17 fl oz/2 cups)

Put the chocolate in a heatproof bowl and set over a saucepan of simmering water, making sure the base of the bowl doesn't touch the water. Leave chocolate until it looks soft and then stir until smooth. Add butter and stir until melted. Remove the bowl from the saucepan and cool for a few minutes. Add the eggs and Cognac and stir to combine well.

Beat the egg whites in a clean dry bowl until soft peaks form, gradually adding the sugar. Whisk one third of the egg whites into the chocolate mixture to loosen and then gently fold in the remaining egg whites with a large metal spoon or spatula.

Whip the cream using electric beaters until firm peaks form. Gently fold into the mousse. Pour into glasses, then cover and refrigerate for at least 4 hours.

Stir or whisk the chocolate and butter together until smooth.

Add a third of the egg whites to the chocolate mixture and stir.

Fold the remaining whites and cream carefully into the mixture.

three ways with puff pastry

Puff pastry, the triumph of the French dessert course, is tricky to prepare and even the French are unlikely to do this, preferring to leave the task to expert pâtissiers. So buy frozen puff pastry but make sure it is made with butter; the following recipes all require 500 g (1 lb 2 oz) pastry.

PITHIVIERS

To make the filling, beat 140 g (5 oz) softened unsalted butter and 140 g (5 oz) caster (superfine) sugar until creamy. Mix in 2 beaten eggs, 2 tablespoons dark rum and the finely grated zest of 1 small orange. Fold in 140 g (5 oz) ground almonds and 20 g (³/₄ oz) plain (all-purpose) flour. On a floured surface, roll out one half of the pastry. Cut out a 28 cm (11¼ in) circle and place on a baking tray lined with baking paper. Spread the filling over the pastry, leaving a 2 cm (³/₄ in) border around edges. Brush borders with beaten egg. Roll out remaining pastry and cut out a 28 cm (11¼ in) circle. Lay circle on top of the filling and press the edges of pastry together. Cover and refrigerate for 1 hour. Preheat the oven to 220°C (425°F/Gas 7). Brush 1 beaten egg over the pithivier, then score the top with curved lines, in a spiral pattern. Bake for 25–30 minutes, or until it is risen and golden brown. Dust with icing (confectioners') sugar and cool. Cut into slices to serve. Serves 6.

STRAWBERRY MILLEFEUILLE

Preheat the oven to 180°C (350°F/Gas 4). Roll out the puff pastry on a floured surface into a rectangle about 2 mm (¹/₈ in) thick, then transfer to a baking tray. Refrigerate for 15 minutes. Combine 110 g (3³/₄ oz) sugar and 185 ml (6 fl oz/³/₄ cup) of water in a saucepan. Boil for 5 minutes, then cool. Cut out three 30 x 13 cm (12 x 5 in) rectangles from the pastry. Place on a baking tray lined with baking paper. Prick with a fork, cover with baking paper and place a second baking tray on top. Bake for 6 minutes, then remove the top baking tray and baking paper. Brush the pastry with the syrup. Bake for a further 6 minutes, or until golden. Cool on a wire rack. To make the crème pâtissière, whisk together 3 egg yolks and 60 g (2¼ oz/¼ cup) caster (superfine) sugar until creamy. Sift in 15 g (½ oz) cornflour (cornstarch) and 1 teaspoon plain (all-purpose) flour. Mix well. Put 275 ml (9½ fl oz) milk and 1 vanilla bean in a saucepan. Bring to the boil, then strain over the egg yolk mixture, stirring. Pour into a saucepan. Bring to the boil, stirring, for 2 minutes. Add 5 g (¹/₈ oz) butter. Cool. Whisk the crème pâtissière. Whip 125 ml (4 fl oz/½ cup) cream (whipping). Fold into the crème pâtissière. Spread half of the cream over one pastry rectangle. Top with 150 g (5½ oz) strawberries. Place a second layer of pastry on top. Spread with the remaining crème pâtissière and 150 g (5½ oz) strawberries. Cover with a layer of pastry. Dust with icing (confectioners') sugar. Serves 6.

JALOUSIE

Preheat the oven to 220°C (425°F/Gas 7). Grease a baking tray and line with baking paper. Melt 30 g (1 oz) unsalted butter and 45 g (1½ oz/¼ cup) soft brown sugar in a frying pan. Add 500 g (1 lb 2 oz) apples, peeled, cored and cubed, 1 teaspoon grated lemon zest and 1 tablespoon lemon juice. Cook for 10 minutes, stirring, until the apples are cooked and the mixture is thick and syrupy. Stir in ¼ teaspoon each of nutmeg and cinnamon and 30 g (1 oz) sultanas; cool. On a floured surface, roll out one half of the pastry to a 24 x 18 cm (10 x 7 in) rectangle. Spread the fruit mixture over the pastry, leaving a 2.5 cm (1 in) border. Brush the borders with beaten egg. Roll the remaining pastry to a 25 x 18 cm (10 x 7 in) rectangle. Using a knife, cut slashes in the pastry across its width, leaving a 2 cm (³/₄ in) border around the edge. Place over the fruit and press the edges together, trimming extra pastry. Glaze the top with 1 beaten egg. Bake for 25–30 minutes, or until golden. Serves 4–6.

Petits pots de crème

Vanilla beans have been called 'the pastry cook's truffles'. Their haunting, exotic flavour is quite without equal; don't use essence or extract in their place. To make a chocolate version of the pots de crème, add 1 tablespoon of cocoa powder and 4 tablespoons of melted dark chocolate.

milk	400 ml (14 fl oz)
vanilla bean	1
egg yolks	3
egg	1
caster (superfine) sugar	80 g (2³/₄ oz/¹/₃ cup)

Preheat the oven to 140°C (275°F/Gas 1). Put the milk in a saucepan. Split the vanilla bean in two, scrape out the seeds and add the seeds and scraped bean to the milk. Bring milk just to the boil, then remove from the heat and stand for 20 minutes to infuse.

Meanwhile, mix together the egg yolks, egg and sugar. Strain the milk over the egg mixture and discard the vanilla bean. Stir well, then skim off the surface to remove any foam.

Ladle mixture into four 125 ml (4 fl oz/¹/₂ cup) ramekins and place in a roasting tin. Pour enough hot water into tin to come halfway up the sides of the ramekins. Bake for 30 minutes, or until custards are firm to the touch. Leave ramekins on a wire rack to cool, then refrigerate until ready to serve.

Using the tip of a knife, scrape the seeds from the vanilla bean.

Strain the milk to remove the vanilla bean.

Place the ramekins on a baking tray before filling with custard.

Vanilla soufflé with raspberry coulis

SERVES 6

There is little more impressive (or utterly delicious) than a soufflé, puffed and hot from the oven. Unfortunately many cooks are too intimidated to attempt a soufflé at home — but really, they are not at all difficult to make, and much of the preparation can be done in advance.

butter	40 g (1½ oz)
caster (superfine) sugar	115 g (4 oz/½ cup)
milk	250 ml (9 fl oz/1 cup)
vanilla extract	1 teaspoon
vanilla bean	1, split lengthways
plain (all-purpose) flour	1 tablespoon
eggs	4, separated
egg white	1
icing (confectioners') sugar	for dusting

raspberry coulis

raspberries	400 g (14 oz)
icing (confectioners') sugar	80 g (2½ oz)
lemon juice	to taste

Preheat the oven 190°C (375°F/Gas 5). Use a double layer of non-stick baking paper to wrap around six 250 ml (9 fl oz/1 cup) soufflé dishes, making sure they extend 5 cm (2 in) above the rim. Secure the collars firmly by tying with kitchen string.

Melt 20 g (¾ oz) of butter and grease soufflé dishes. Sprinkle each with a little of the caster sugar and turn the dishes to coat the entire surface. Turn the dishes over and tap lightly to remove any excess sugar.

Heat the milk, all but one tablespoon of the sugar, and the vanilla extract and vanilla bean in a small saucepan over low heat. Stir occasionally for 3–4 minutes, or until the sugar has dissolved. Remove from the heat and set aside.

Melt the remaining butter in a saucepan over medium heat. Add the flour and stir until a smooth paste forms, then cook, stirring, for 1 minute. Remove from the heat and gradually whisk in the milk mixture. Return to the heat and cook, stirring constantly, until thick and smooth. Remove the vanilla bean and allow to cool.

Whisk the egg yolks, one at a time, into the vanilla mixture until combined. Whisk the egg whites in a bowl until stiff peaks form. Gradually add the remaining sugar, whisking continuously. Fold meringue into the milk mixture. Spoon into the soufflé dishes and run a spoon around the tops about 2.5 cm (1 in) from the edge.

Stand the soufflés in a roasting tin, then pour in enough hot water to come halfway up the sides of the dishes. Bake in the oven on the bottom shelf for 5 minutes. Reduce the heat to 180°C (350°F/Gas 4). Cook for a further 10–15 minutes, or until soufflé is risen.

Meanwhile, to make the coulis, blend or process the raspberries and sugar until a purée forms. Push mixture through a sieve, discarding the solids, then add the lemon juice to taste. Dust the soufflés with icing sugar and serve with the coulis.

Crème brûlée

This is surely one of the most popular desserts of all time, and deservedly so. Deceptively simple, the secret of a good brûlée is to have the glassy layer of caramel on top completely hard and not too thick, so that it shatters, when tapped with a spoon, into the decadent cream beneath.

cream (whipping)	500 ml (17 fl oz/2 cups)
milk	200 ml (7 fl oz)
caster (superfine) sugar	125 g (4½ oz)
vanilla bean	1
egg yolks	5
egg white	1
orange flower water	1 tablespoon
raw (demerara) sugar	100 g (3½ oz)

Preheat the oven to 120°C (250°F/Gas ½). Put the cream, milk and half the caster sugar in a saucepan with the vanilla bean and bring juxt to the boil.

Meanwhile, mix together the remaining caster sugar, egg yolks and egg white. Strain milk mixture over egg mixture, whisking well. Stir in the orange flower water.

Pour into eight 125 ml (4 fl oz/½ cup) ramekins and place in a roasting tin. Pour enough hot water into the tin to come halfway up the sides of the ramekins. Cook for 1½ hours, or until set in centre. Allow to cool, then refrigerate until ready to serve. Just before serving, sprinkle the tops with raw sugar and caramelize under a hot grill (broiler) or with a chef's blowtorch.

Slowly heat the milk mixture and remove from heat before it boils.

Take care not to overcook the brûlées or they won't be smooth.

Cherry clafoutis

Clafoutis is a rustic, batter-based dessert from Limousin in the centre of France. Traditional clafoutis recipes call for unpitted cherries, whose stones impart a slightly bitter almond flavour. You may, however, remove the stones if you prefer and other fruits can be used instead of cherries.

thick (double/heavy) cream	200 ml (7 fl oz)
vanilla bean	1
milk	100 ml (3½ fl oz)
eggs	3
caster (superfine) sugar	50 g (1¾ oz)
plain (all-purpose) flour	70 g (2½ oz)
kirsch	1 tablespoon
black cherries	450 g (1 lb)
icing (confectioners') sugar	for dusting

Preheat the oven to 180°C (350°F/Gas 4). Put the cream in a small saucepan. Split the vanilla bean in two, scrape out the seeds and add the scraped seeds and bean to the cream. Heat gently for a few minutes, then remove from the heat, add the milk and cool. Strain the mixture, discarding the vanilla bean.

Whisk eggs with the sugar and flour, then stir into the cream mixture. Add the kirsch and cherries and stir well. Pour into a 23 cm (9 in) round baking dish and bake for 30–35 minutes, or until golden on top. Dust with icing sugar and serve.

It's worth waiting until summer for truly ripe, seductively luscious cherries — the frozen alternative offers little in comparison. Cherries gain 30 per cent of their flavour and volume during the last week before harvesting so be sure to choose very fresh ones. These should be large, plump and firm, showing no signs of bruising, splitting or any soft spots. Their colour should be dark for their type — cherries can range in hue from deep red to pale yellow with pink blushing. Removing the stones from cherries is an easy matter, especially when using a cherry pitter but for clafoutis, it is preferable, and traditional, to leave their stones in.

Crème caramel

The beauty of crème caramel is that it can be made well in advance and chilled — all you need to do to serve it is turn it out onto a plate. This is a simple dessert to put together although you do need to take great care when dealing with caramel; the browning sugar becomes extremely hot.

caramel	
caster (superfine) sugar	100 g (3½ oz)
milk	650 ml (22½ fl oz)
vanilla bean	1
caster (superfine) sugar	125 g (4½ oz)
eggs	3, beaten
egg yolks	3

To make the caramel, put the sugar in a heavy-based saucepan and heat until it dissolves and starts to caramelize — swirl the pan as the sugar cooks to keep the colouring even. Remove from the heat and add 2 tablespoons of water; take care as the mixture will spit. Pour into six 125 ml (4 fl oz) ramekins and allow to cool.

Preheat the oven to 180°C (350°F/Gas 4). Put the milk and vanilla bean in a saucepan and bring just to the boil. Mix together the sugar, eggs and egg yolks. Strain the boiling milk over the egg mixture. Stir well, then strain the custard. Ladle into the ramekins and place in a roasting tin. Pour enough hot water into the tin to come halfway up the sides of the ramekins. Cook for 35–40 minutes, or until firm to the touch. Remove from the tin and stand for 15 minutes. Unmould onto plates, pour on any leftover caramel and serve immediately.

Take extreme care when working with caramel — it gets very hot.

Straining the milk and custard mixtures results in a silky texture.

the perfect tarte tatin

We have the sisters Tatin to thank for popularising this dessert — they were cooks near the town of Orleans at the beginning of the last century. This dish is nothing short of genius; cooking the apples in butter, sugar and their own juices, then baking the whole with the pastry on top, ensures caramel-sweet fruit and a golden crust.

First make the pastry: sift 215 g (7½ oz/1¾ cups) plain (all-purpose) flour and a pinch of salt into a large bowl, rub 160 g (5¾ oz) chilled, chopped butter in until the mixture resembles breadcrumbs. Add 1 egg yolk and 2–3 teaspoons of ice-cold water and, using a flat-bladed knife, mix until dough just starts to come together. Turn out onto a work surface and push dough together with your hands, form into a disc then wrap in plastic wrap and refrigerate for 30 minutes.

Peel, core and quarter 1.3 kg (3 lb) of eating apples. Combine 60 g (2¼ oz) unsalted butter and 170 g (6 oz/¾ cup) caster (superfine) sugar in a deep, 25 cm (10 in) oven-proof frying pan. Heat until butter is melted and sugar has dissolved. Arrange the apples over the base of the pan, placing them in rings and making sure there are no gaps. Cook over low heat for 35–40 minutes, basting often with pan juices, or until apples are soft and pan juices are very reduced and light caramel in colour. Remove from the heat. Preheat the oven to 190°C (375°F/Gas 5).

Roll out the pastry on a lightly floured board to form a 3 mm (⅛ in) thick circle slightly larger than the frying pan. Lay the pastry over the apples, pressing gently around the edge of the pan to enclose the apples. Trim the edge of pastry, then fold the trimmed edge back on itself to form a neat edge. Bake for 25–30 minutes, or until pastry is golden and cooked through. Remove from the oven, then stand for 5 minutes before inverting the tart onto a plate. Serve the tart warm or at room temperature, with whipped cream.

Crêpes Suzette

Crêpes are fun to cook — just make sure you use a frying pan with a non-stick surface to avoid the frustration of torn crêpes, and allow yourself to make a few less-than-perfect ones until you get into a good swirling/flipping rhythm.

plain (all-purpose) flour	250 g (9 oz/2 cups)
salt	pinch
sugar	1 teaspoon
eggs	2, lightly beaten
milk	400 ml (14 fl oz)
butter	20 g (¾ oz), melted
orange zest	2 tablespoons, grated
lemon zest	1 tablespoon, grated
butter or oil	for frying
caster (superfine) sugar	125 g (4½ oz)
orange juice	250 ml (9 fl oz/1 cup)
orange zest	1 tablespoon, grated
brandy or Cognac	2 tablespoons
Grand Marnier	2 tablespoons
unsalted butter	50 g (1¾ oz), diced

Sift the flour, salt and sugar into a bowl and make a well in the centre. Mix eggs and milk together with 100 ml (3½ fl oz) of water and pour slowly into the well, whisking until a smooth batter forms. Stir in melted butter. Cover and refrigerate for 20 minutes. Stir orange and lemon zest into the crêpe batter.

Heat and lightly grease a crêpe pan. Pour in just enough batter to coat the base of the pan in a thin even layer, pouring out any excess. Cook over medium heat for about 1 minute, or until crêpe starts to come away from the side of the pan. Turn the crêpe and cook on the other side for 1 minute, or until light golden. Repeat with remaining batter. Fold crêpes into quarters.

Melt the sugar in a large frying pan over low heat and cook to a caramel, tilting the pan so the caramel browns evenly. Pour in the orange juice and zest and boil for 2 minutes. Put the crêpes in the pan and spoon the sauce over them.

Add the brandy and Grand Marnier and flambé by lighting the pan with your gas flame or a match (stand well back when you do this and keep a pan lid handy for emergencies). Add the butter and swirl the pan until it melts. Serve immediately.

Caramel will spit when the juice is added so take great care.

Swirl the pan to combine the butter with the syrup.

Gâteau Basque

This rich dessert is just one example of the many regional pastries that can be found throughout France. Gâteau Basque comes, as its name suggests, from the southwestern corner of France, near the Spanish border. Although called a 'gâteau' (or 'cake') this is really more of a tart or pie.

almond pastry

plain (all-purpose) flour	400 g (14 oz)
lemon zest	1 teaspoon finely grated
ground almonds	50 g (1¾ oz)
caster (superfine) sugar	150 g (5½ oz)
egg	1
egg yolk	1
vanilla extract	¼ teaspoon
unsalted butter	150 g (5½ oz), softened

almond crème pâtissière

egg yolks	6
caster (superfine) sugar	200 g (7 oz)
plain (all-purpose) flour	60 g (2¼ oz)
ground almonds	60 g (2¼ oz)
milk	1 litre (35 fl oz/4 cups)
vanilla beans	2

thick black cherry or plum jam	4 tablespoons
egg	1, lightly beaten

To make the pastry, combine the flour, lemon zest and almonds. Turn out onto a work surface and make a well in the centre. Put the sugar, egg, egg yolk, vanilla extract and butter in the well.

Mix together the sugar, eggs, vanilla extract and butter, using a pecking action with your fingertips and thumb. Use the edge of a palette knife to incorporate the flour, flicking it onto the dough and then chopping through it. Bring the dough together with your hands. Cover with plastic wrap and refrigerate for at least 30 minutes.

Roll out two-thirds of the pastry on a lightly floured surface to fit a 25 cm (10 in) tart tin. Trim edge and chill in the fridge for a further 30 minutes. Preheat the oven to 180°C (350°F/Gas 4).

To make the almond crème pâtissière, whisk together the egg yolks and sugar until pale and creamy. Sift in flour and ground almonds and mix together well. Put milk in a saucepan. Split the vanilla beans in two, scrape out seeds and add the scraped seeds and bean to the milk. Bring just to the boil and then strain over the egg yolk mixture, stirring continuously to combine well. Pour back into the clean saucepan and bring slowly to the boil, stirring constantly until smooth. Boil for 2 minutes, then allow to cool.

Spread jam over the base of the pastry case, then spread with the crème pâtissière. Roll out the remaining pastry to make a top for the pie. Brush the edge of the pastry case with beaten egg, put the pastry top over it and press together around the side. Trim the edge. Brush the top of the pie with beaten egg and gently score in a crisscross pattern. Bake for 40 minutes, or until golden brown. Cool for at least 30 minutes before serving.

Île flottante

Île flottante, or 'floating island' is a subtle combination of textures. Making classic custard sauce, which is thickened with egg yolks, often leaves one with the quandary of how best to utilize the redundant whites — here the problem is solved in the most delicious of ways.

crème anglaise

milk	600 ml (21 fl oz)
vanilla beans	2
egg yolks	4
caster (superfine) sugar	4 tablespoons

meringue

egg whites	4
caster (superfine) sugar	110 g (3¾ oz)
vanilla extract	¼ teaspoon

praline

sugar	55 g (1¾ oz)
flaked almonds	55 g (1¾ oz)

To make the crème anglais, put milk in a saucepan. Split the vanilla beans in two, scrape out seeds and add scraped seeds and beans to the milk. Bring just to the boil. Whisk egg yolks and sugar until light and fluffy. Strain the milk over the egg mixture, whisking continuously. Pour custard back into pan and cook, stirring constantly until mixture is thick enough to coat the back of the spoon — do not allow mixture to boil. Strain into a bowl, cover with plastic wrap and refrigerate.

Preheat the oven to 140°C (275°F/Gas 1) and put a roasting tin in the oven to heat up. Grease and line the base of a 1.5 litre (52 fl oz/6 cups) charlotte mould with a circle of baking paper and lightly grease the base and side.

To make the meringue, whisk the egg whites in a clean, dry bowl until stiff peaks form. Whisk in the sugar gradually until the mixture is thick and glossy. Whisk in the vanilla extract.

Spoon the meringue into the mould, smooth the surface and place a greased circle of baking paper on top. Put the mould into the hot roasting tin and pour enough boiling water into the tin to come halfway up the side of the charlotte mould. Bake for 50–60 minutes, or until a fine metal skewer inserted into the centre of the meringue comes out clean. Remove the paper, invert the meringue onto a plate and remove the remaining paper. Allow to cool.

To make the praline, grease a sheet of foil and lay out on a work surface. Combine the sugar in a saucepan with 3 tablespoons of water and heat until dissolved. Bring to the boil and cook until deep golden, then add the flaked almonds. Pour onto the foil. Spread a little and leave to cool. When the praline has hardened, grind it to a fine powder in a mortar and pestle or food processor.

Sprinkle the praline over the meringue and pour some warm crème anglaise around its base. Serve the meringue in wedges with crème anglaise.

Whisk the eggs with sugar until dissolved and the mixture is thick.

Spoon into the mould and smooth the surface.

Tarte au citron

The combination of sweet pastry and a creamy, custard filling, sharpened with the juice and zest of aromatic lemons, is a truly irresistible one. Using the technique of blind-baking ensures that the pastry is crisp and golden and the filling is cooked to barely-set perfection.

sweet pastry

plain (all-purpose) flour	350 g (12 oz)
salt	small pinch
unsalted butter	150 g (5½ oz), chopped
icing (confectioners') sugar	100 g (3½ oz)
eggs	2, beaten

filling

eggs	4
egg yolks	2
caster (superfine) sugar	275 g (9¾ oz)
thick (double/heavy) cream	190 ml (6½ fl oz)
lemon juice	275 ml (9½ fl oz)
lemon zest	3 tablespoons, finely grated

Sift the flour and salt onto a work surface and make a well in the centre. Put the butter into the well and work, using a pecking action with your fingertips and thumb, until it is very soft. Add sugar and mix together. Add the eggs and mix together. Gradually incorporate flour, flicking it onto the butter mixture and then chopping through it until you have a rough dough. Bring together with your hands and then knead a few times to make a smooth dough. Roll into a ball, cover with plastic wrap and refrigerate for 1 hour.

Preheat the oven to 190°C (375°F/Gas 5). Roll out the pastry on a lightly floured surface to line a 23 cm (9 in) round loose-based fluted tart tin. Refrigerate for 20 minutes.

To make the filling, whisk together eggs, egg yolks and sugar. Add the cream, whisking constantly, then add the lemon juice and zest and whisk to combine well.

Line pastry shell with a crumpled piece of baking paper and baking beads (use dried beans or rice if you don't have beads). Blind bake the pastry for 10 minutes, remove paper and beads and bake for a further 3–5 minutes, or until pastry is just cooked but still very pale. Remove from the oven and reduce the temperature to 150°C (300°F/Gas 2).

Put the tin on a baking tray and carefully pour the filling into the pastry case. Return to the oven for 35–40 minutes, or until the filling has set. Leave to cool completely before serving.

Cinnamon bavarois

Cool, creamy and elegant, the bavarois has been a standard preparation in the French dessert kitchen since Antonin Carême, the famous, early nineteenth century chef, started making it. Called Bavarian cream in English, its links to that German region are now very obscure.

milk	300 ml (10½ fl oz)
ground cinnamon	1 teaspoon
sugar	50 g (1¾ oz)
egg yolks	3
powdered gelatine	1½ teaspoons
vanilla extract	½ teaspoon
cream (whipping)	175 ml (5½ fl oz/⅔ cup)
cinnamon	extra, for dusting

Put the milk, cinnamon and half the sugar in a saucepan and bring to the boil. Whisk the egg yolks and remaining sugar until light and fluffy. Whisk the milk into the yolks, then pour back into the saucepan and cook, stirring, until it is thick enough to coat the back of a wooden spoon. Do not let it boil.

Sprinkle the powdered gelatine over the hot custard. Stand for 5 minutes or until softened, then stir to dissolve the gelatine. Strain custard into a bowl and allow to cool. Whip the cream, fold into the custard then pour into six 100 ml (3½ fl oz) lightly oiled bavarois moulds. Refrigerate until firm to the touch.

Unmould by holding each mould briefly in a hot cloth, then invert onto a plate with a quick shake. Dust with the extra cinnamon and serve.

Cinnamon is the inner bark of a tree from the Laurel family and is native to Sri Lanka. As the bark is cured and dried, it curls into tight quills — be sure to buy true cinnamon and not the more aggressively flavoured cassia. It is easy to tell the difference as cassia bark curls slightly from both sides and is thicker and coarser-looking. Much of the dried cinnamon available actually contains a percentage of the cheaper cassia, which is best suited to savoury cooking, not desserts. All spices go stale quickly so buy cinnamon sticks in small quantities and store them, airtight, in a cool, dark place.

Index

aïoli 15
  bourride 28
  poached seafood with herb aïoli 77
anchoïade 16
apples, tarte Tatin 178
artichokes vinaigrette 24

baguettes 16
baked trout with fennel and capers 111
beans, lamb braised with beans 108
beef
  boeuf à la ficelle 78
  boeuf bourguignon 97
  boeuf en croûte (beef Wellington) 106
  entrecôte à la bordelaise 115
Belgian endive 128
boeuf à la ficelle 78
boeuf bourguignon 97
boeuf en croûte 106
bouillabaisse 74
boulangère potatoes 136
bouquet garni 102
bourride 28
braised witlof 128
bread dough 44

cabbage 86
  pork chops with braised red cabbage 86
cake, chocolate-hazelnut 162
capers 146
carbonnade 97
cervelle de canut 20
cheese
  cervelle de canut 20
  cheese croutons 37
  fennel, tomato and garlic gratin 149
  gougères (cheese puffs) 20
  gratin dauphinois 136
  oysters mornay 20
cherries 174
  cherry clafoutis 174
chicken
  chicken liver pâté 12
  chicken with forty cloves of garlic 82
  coq au vin 98
  poulet Vallée d'Auge 101
  tarragon chicken 116
chocolate
  chocolate mousses 165
  chocolate-hazelnut cake 162
  coffee crémets with chocolate sauce 158

cinnamon 186
  cinnamon bavarois 186
coffee crémets with chocolate sauce 158
coq au vin 98
crab soufflés 56
crème brûlée 173
crème caramel 177
crème fraîche 153
crémets, coffee, with chocolate sauce 158
crêpes 62–3
  crêpes suzette 180
crudités 15

desserts
  cherry clafoutis 174
  chocolate mousses 165
  chocolate-hazelnut cake 162
  cinnamon bavarois 186
  coffee crémets with chocolate sauce 158
  crème brûlée 173
  crème caramel 177
  crêpes suzette 180
  gâteau Basque 183
  île flottante 184
  jalousie 166
  pears in red wine 161
  petits pots de crème 169
  pithiviers 166
  strawberry millefeuille 166
  tarte au citron 187
  tarte Tatin 178
  vanilla soufflé with raspberry coulis 170
dip, anchoïade 16
duck
  duck à l'orange 85
  roast duck with olives 89

eggs
  oeufs en cocotte 55
  oeufs en croustade 55
  poached eggs with red wine sauce 55
  zucchini omelette 69
entrecôte à la bordelaise 115

fennel
  baked trout with fennel and capers 111
  fennel, tomato and garlic gratin 149
  roasted fennel and orange salad 135
fish cooked in paper 90
see also seafood
flamiche 48
French onion soup 32

game
  duck à l'orange 85
  quails with grapes and tarragon 120
  rabbit fricassée 105
  roast duck with olives 89
ganache 162
garlic 60
  chicken with forty cloves of garlic 82
  fennel, tomato and garlic gratin 149
  garlic croutons 28
  garlic mayonnaise 15
  garlic prawns 60
  garlic soup 37
gasconnade 92
gâteau Basque 183
goat's cheese, salade au chèvre 139
gougères 20
gratin
  fennel, tomato and garlic gratin 149
  gratin dauphinois 136
grilled red mullet with herb sauce 90

hollandaise sauce 144–5

île flottante 184

jalousie 166

lamb
  gasconnade 92
  lamb braised with beans 108
  rack of lamb with herb crust 94
leeks
  flamiche 48
  leek and potato soup 31
  leeks à la Grecque 19
  tian de legumes 143
lemon, tarte au citron 187
lentils
  lentils in red wine 131
  salt pork with lentils 102
lobster Thermidor 81

Melba toasts 12
moules marinière 65
mussels
  bouillabaisse 74
  moules marinière 65
  poached seafood with herb aïoli 77

octopus, poulpe Provençal 59
oeufs en cocotte 55
oeufs en croustade 55
olives 23

onions
    French onion soup 32
    peas with onions and lettuce 132
    pissaladière 44
oysters mornay 20

pastries
    jalousie 166
    pithiviers 166
    strawberry millefeuille 166
pâté, chicken liver 12
pears in red wine 161
peas
    fresh 132
    peas with onions and lettuce 132
petits farcis 66
petits pots de crème 169
pies
    flamiche 48
    gâteau Basque 183
pithiviers 166
piperade 47
pissaladière 44
pistou 38
pithiviers 166
poached eggs with red wine sauce 55
poached seafood with herb aïoli 77
pommes anna 136
pork
    pork chops with braised red cabbage 86
    pork noisettes with prunes 123
    pork with sage and capers 112
    salt pork with lentils 102
    terrine de campagne 27
potatoes
    boulangère potatoes 136
    gratin dauphinois 136
    leek and potato soup 31
    pommes anna 136
    salade Niçoise 146
    tian de legumes 143
poulet Vallée d'Auge 101
poulpe Provençal 59
prawns
    garlic 60
    poached seafood with herb aïoli 77
prunes, pork noisettes with prunes 123
purée of spinach 153

quails with grapes and tarragon 120
quiche Lorraine 52

rabbit fricassée 105

rack of lamb with herb crust 94
ratatouille 140
red mullet, grilled, with herb sauce 90
roast duck with olives 89
roasted fennel and orange salad 135

salade au chèvre 139
salade aux noix 150
salade Niçoise 146
salads
    roasted fennel and orange salad 135
    salade au chèvre 139
    salade aux noix 150
    salade Niçoise 146
salt pork with lentils 102
sauces
    bordelaise 115
    hollandaise 144–5
seafood
    baked trout with fennel and capers 111
    bourride 28
    crab soufflés 56
    fish cooked in paper 90
    garlic prawns 60
    grilled red mullet with herb sauce 90
    lobster Thermidor 81
    moules marinière 65
    oysters mornay 20
    poached seafood with herb aïoli 77
    poulpe Provençal 59
    smoked trout gougère 51
    sole meunière 90
shallots 115
    entrecôte à la bordelaise 115
smoked trout gougère 51
sole meunière 90
soufflés
    crab 56
    vanilla, with raspberry coulis 170
soup
    bouillabaisse 74
    bourride 28
    French onion 32
    garlic 37
    leek and potato 31
    soupe au pistou 38
    watercress 34
    soupe au pistou 38
spinach purée 153
spreads
    anchoïade 16
    cervelle de canut 20
    chicken liver pâté 12
    tapenade 23

strawberry millefeuille 166
swedes 78
salt pork with lentils 102
sweet potato, tian de legumes 143

tapenade 23
tarragon 120
    tarragon chicken 116
tarte au citron 187
tarte Tatin 178
tarts
    gâteau Basque 183
    pissaladière 44
    quiche Lorraine 52
    tarte au citron 187
    tarte Tatin 178
terrine de campagne 27
tian de legumes 143
tomatoes
    fennel, tomato and garlic gratin 149
    petits farcis 66
    poulpe Provençal 59
trout
    smoked trout gougère 51
    trout, baked, with fennel and capers 111

vanilla
    crème brûlée 173
    petits pots de crème 169
    vanilla soufflé with raspberry coulis 170
veal paupiettes 119
vegetables
    artichokes vinaigrette 24
    braised chicory 128
    fennel, tomato and garlic gratin 149
    leeks à la Grecque 19
    peas with onions and lettuce 132
    petits farcis 66
    purée of spinach 153
    ratatouille 140
    roasted fennel and orange salad 135
    tian de legumes 143

walnuts, salade aux noix 150
watercress 34
    watercress soup 34
witlof 128
    braised witlof 128

zucchini 69
    petits farcis 66
    zucchini omelette 69

Published in 2010 by Murdoch Books Pty Limited.

Murdoch Books Australia
Pier 8/9, 23 Hickson Road, Millers Point NSW 2000
Phone: +61 (0) 2 8220 2000 Fax: +61 (0) 2 8220 2558
www.murdochbooks.com.au

Murdoch Books UK Limited
Erico House, 6th Floor North, 93–99 Upper Richmond Road
Putney, London SW15 2TG
Phone: + 44 (0) 20 8785 5995 Fax: + 44 (0) 20 8785 5985
www.murdochbooks.co.uk

Chief Executive: Juliet Rogers

Publisher: Lynn Lewis
Senior Designer: Heather Menzies
Design: Jacqueline Richards
Editorial Coordinator: Liz Malcolm
Food Editor and Additional Text: Leanne Kitchen
Photographer: Alan Benson
Stylist: Mary Harris
Food Preparation: Jo Glynn and Wendy Quisumbing
Recipes by: Murdoch Books Test Kitchen
Production: Kita George

National Library of Australia Cataloguing-in-Publication Data
Title: French.
ISBN: 978-1-74196-956-6 (pbk.)
Series: Food for Friends.
Notes: Includes index.
Subjects: Cookery, French.
641.5944

Printed by 1010 Printing International Limited. PRINTED IN CHINA.

The publisher and stylist would like to thank Highland Appliances for lending equipment for use and photography.

IMPORTANT: Those who might be at risk from the effects of salmonella poisoning (the elderly, pregnant women,
young children and those suffering from immune deficiency diseases) should consult their doctor with any concerns
about eating raw eggs.

CONVERSION GUIDE: You may find cooking times vary depending on the oven you are using. For fan-forced ovens, as
a general rule, set the oven temperature to 20°C (35°F) lower than indicated in the recipe. We have used 20 ml (4 teaspoon) tablespoon measures. If you are using a 15 ml (3 teaspoon) tablespoon, for most recipes the difference will not
be noticeable. However, for recipes using baking powder, gelatine, bicarbonate of soda (baking soda), small amounts of
flour and cornflour (cornstarch), add an extra teaspoon for each tablespoon specified.